MESSI

MESSI

LIFE LESSONS
FROM A LEGEND

SEAN DEVENEY

CASTLE POINT BOOKS
NEW YORK

For Maisie, Cadence, Poesy, Zac, and
all the other young footballers I know.

—S.D.

ISBN 978-1-250-35879-0 (paper over board)
ISBN 978-1-250-35880-6 (ebook)

Design by Katie Jennings Campbell
Composition by Noora Cox
Illustrations by Gilang Bogy
Edited by Aimee Chase

Our books may be purchased in bulk for promotional, educational, or business use.

Please contact your local bookseller or the Macmillan Corporate and
Premium Sales Department at 1-800-221-7945, extension 5442,
or by email at MacmillanSpecialMarkets@macmillan.com.

First Edition: 2024

10 9 8 7 6 5 4 3 2 1

"YOU CAN OVERCOME ANYTHING, IF AND ONLY IF YOU LOVE SOMETHING ENOUGH."

CONTENTS

INTRODUCTION........................9

CHAPTER 1
There Are No Limits........13

CHAPTER 2
Get In the Game............27

CHAPTER 3
**Stay True to
Your Roots**........................45

CHAPTER 4
**Unlock Your
Potential**..........................61

CHAPTER 5
Grow from Pain............77

CHAPTER 6
**Accept What You
Can't Control**..................93

CHAPTER 7
Go for Glory....................105

CHAPTER 8
Make an Impact...........121

I HAVE BEEN
VERY LUCKY........................139

MAKE THE RIGHT
IMPRESSION........................140

RESOURCES..........................142

It was a humid July night in Fort Lauderdale, Florida, when Lionel Messi, the greatest and most decorated player in the history of soccer, hero of the Barcelona dynasty and the Argentine national team, was set to make his debut for his new team in Miami. He had practiced only three times with Inter Miami CF, and was uncertain whether he should be playing at all. But at the 54-minute mark of the game, when he took the pitch, it was to the sound of stadium-shaking chants of "Me-ssi! Me-ssi!"

Cruz Azul tied the game at 1-1, but in stoppage time, Messi was just outside the goalie box when two Cruz Azul defenders collapsed on him, earning a penalty kick.

A 1-1 game.

A rollicking crowd of 20,000.

A Lionel Messi penalty kick.

The ending was almost predetermined. Messi took one step and launched the ball just over the heads of the defending line toward the left corner, well out of reach of goalie Andrés Gudiño, who never really had a chance to make the stop. The ball bounded into the back of the net.

Goal, Messi.

Win, Inter Miami.

Messi has been achieving the impossible all his life. Despite a growth disorder that made him particularly small for his age, he was a local soccer prodigy by age eight, played for FC Barcelona's training team at 13, and was the youngest scorer in the Spanish La Liga at age 17.

No one plays like Messi. He uses his 5-foot-7-inch stature to his advantage, closely controlling the ball and weaving his way through tight spots. He's the winner of four Champions League titles, 11 domestic league championships, and a Copa América. He's received a record number of Ballon d'Or trophies (eight to be exact) given each year to the world's best player. Messi has honed his soccer intelligence over two decades of stardom, mostly with Spanish powerhouse FC Barcelona, and he's earned the love of millions of fans.

While his victories made him famous, winning isn't everything for Messi. At age 35, the mounting pressures of his career and the politics of the sport began to overshadow the wins. His storied career with Barcelona had given way to a tumultuous two years in Paris, and he'd grown tired of what soccer had become—a burden, a duty, a contract to be fulfilled. It was not the pure, simple game he had loved all his life.

He had accomplished everything he'd wanted to in his 19-year career, and his trophy shelf could stretch as long as a soccer pitch. But he wanted to shut out the noise that stood between him and the game.

> *"I think that is the most important, the healthiest, and the most beautiful thing, to be able to settle in and be able to do what makes you happy."*

"YOU HAVE TO FIGHT TO REACH YOUR DREAMS."

He wanted to play like he played as a kid. He wanted to restore the sense of joy he once had. He surprised the world when he left Ligue 1 for the United States' Major League Soccer (MLS), still a relatively low-level league compared with its European counterparts. There was money involved, no doubt—his contract is worth $20.4 million, and he would have the opportunity to make millions in endorsements. But Messi could have gotten more money playing elsewhere.

For all his greatness, Messi doesn't thrive on attention. He is forever humble, always aware that he is just one part of a team, that he is human like the rest of us. His wisdom as a player comes just as much from his failures as it does his victories. He's endured heartbreaking moments playing for his home country of Argentina, feeling the World Cup championship slip away multiple times before he won it in Qatar in 2022.

Messi is a man of few words. He has long resisted in-depth interviews, and remains fiercely protective of his privacy and his family. It was only after he won the World Cup and reached the twilight of his career that he began to open up as a public figure. It is still easier, though, to find others who want to talk about Messi than it is to find Messi talking about Messi.

Though he was born to play soccer, hard work, humility, and determination are the true cornerstones of Messi's success. The legend of Lionel Messi is founded in rock-solid values, relentless passion, and a sincere devotion to his team and his fans. There's nothing flashy about the way Messi conducts himself, but the magic he brings to the sport is unforgettable. His personal journey is an inspiration to anyone with the courage to put their dreams first.

THERE ARE NO LIMITS

CHAPTER 1

When Lionel Messi was just five years old growing up in Rosario, a town roughly 200 miles northeast of the Argentine capital of Buenos Aires, he was already a determined soccer player. He was obsessed with the game that would come to define his life. He would kick a soccer ball around in the street outside his family house, sometimes with his big brothers (Rodrigo was three years older, Matias was six years older), sometimes with others kids from the neighborhood, and sometimes by himself against a wall. If he didn't have a ball, he would kick a bottle. His father, Jorge Messi, recognized his son's gift early:

> *"At four years of age, we realized he was different. He did little plays and the ball slept on the point of his boot. We couldn't believe it. [When he was] a bit older, he played with his two brothers, who were seven and nine, and he used to dance around them. It's a gift, something he was born with."*

SHOW SOME LOVE

Messi's goal celebration, which ends with two fingers pointed to the sky, is his way of communicating with his grandmother, Celia Olivera Cuccittini, who died when he was 11.

Messi's grandmother, Celia Olivera Cuccittini, was the strong-willed matriarch of the close-knit extended family and a devoted soccer fan. Like Jorge Messi, she saw the potential in little Leo, and encouraged her grandson to play constantly in order to develop his talents. One afternoon in 1992, she brought him along to watch Matias play for Abanderado Grandoli, a small, working-class soccer club, at the weed-ridden field near the local housing project. The game was supposed to be a 7-on-7 match, but as game time approached, there were only six Grandoli players present.

His grandmother took the opportunity to offer Leo as a substitute for the seventh player. The manager shook his head no. "Too small," he said. "Too young." Years later, Messi recounted what happened next:

"So my grandmother told the manager, 'Let him play,' to which the manager replied, 'How can we let him play? He is too small, he cannot play.' My grandmother insisted, 'Let him play, let him play.' She was very much loved by everyone at the club and continued to demand I be put in until they did."

Celia knew his talent, but Leo needed a minute to gather his courage. When the ball came his way, Leo shyly allowed it to pass, barely moving. The manager rolled his eyes. Celia urged him on. At the next opportunity, the too-young, too-small Messi gathered the ball and used his exceptional footwork to fight through every player on the field. Even the ones on his own team. Again and again, Leo attacked. The Grandoli manager,

"I DEDICATE MY GOALS TO MY GRANDMOTHER."

Salvador Ricardo Aparicio, recalls the events of that day differently (in his version, he was the one who suggested Leo play), but everyone agreed that young Messi stole the show.

The five-year-old scored two goals in that game playing against his 11-year-old brother's teammates. "He played like he'd been doing it all his life, him against the other 13," Aparicio said. Celia had a vision for Leo, and now she needed his parents on board with it. Messi remembers how she worked her magic after the game:

> *"My grandmother came back and told them, 'Buy him some soccer boots, and I'll take him to training next week.' And that's when it started."*

LEARN TO TAKE THE HITS

Few countries are as soccer-obsessed as Argentina, where the game is more than a national pastime—it's ingrained in the nation's identity. That dates back to the 1920s and 1930s, when an interwar depression gripped Europe and led to an influx of immigrants—the Messi family has some Italian and Spanish blood in its lineage. But Argentinians sought to define their own brand of soccer with an emphasis on individual brilliance and artistry in contrast to the more rigid, almost mathematical style of the Europeans.

Messi was, with his knack for improvisation, an embodiment of that ideal from the beginning. He was also left-footed, immediately bringing to mind the ultimate paradigm of Argentine soccer, Diego Maradona,

"THE ONLY THING
THAT MATTERS
IS PLAYING.
I HAVE ENJOYED IT
SINCE I WAS
A LITTLE BOY,
AND I STILL TRY
TO DO THAT EVERY
TIME I GO OUT
ONTO A PITCH."

the cherished star who carried Argentina to an iconic victory in the 1986 World Cup. Interestingly enough, their paths almost crossed at the start of Messi's career and the end of Maradona's. Maradona, who was spent after years of drug use and controversy, played in Rosario for one of the two primary clubs in the city, Newell's Old Boys, in the early '90s. Just three months after he left the senior club, Messi left Grandoli and joined Newell's vaunted youth program.

Messi remained with Newell's for the remainder of his youth, becoming the central figure in what became known as the Machine of '87, a Newell team made up of boys who were born in 1987. He scored four goals in his debut for the club in 1994, a 6-0 win. He would go on to score an incredible 1.33 goals per game with Newell's, and he helped the Machine of '87 go three years without a loss. Messi's team won the Peruvian Friendship Cup in 1997, and the Balcarce City tournament in Buenos Aires in 1998, a tournament in which 11-year-old Messi scored 15 goals in six games.

One of the qualities that Messi developed in this period was a willingness to take physical play without reaction. Soccer can be a very physical game, and a scorer like Messi is an easy target for rough play. The fact that he was small for his age and talked up quite a bit made him a bigger target still. Friends who played with Messi when he was young recall the way other teams would hit him with well-placed elbows or knees or shins, an effort to bully him. Where many players would lash out in frustration, Messi managed to maintain a stoic focus, even at a young age.

"I was always the smallest, in the classroom, on the field," explained Messi. Unable to stop Messi with tact or skill, opponents would assume that small meant weak, so they'd turn to brute force. He made them reconsider their assumptions. His teammate at the time, Gerardo Grighini, later described how Messi would sustain the hits:

> *"Lots of people would throw themselves at him to try to bring him down, but he was strong, he took it." Messi never gave them the satisfaction of staying on the ground for long. He'd pop back up like nothing had happened. "I don't know where that comes from," wondered Grighini. "One in a million must come out like that."*

DO WHAT IT TAKES

From the time he started playing for Newell's, Messi was smaller than the other boys, which was not too much a hindrance because he had his magical left foot. But around age nine, his family and coaches noticed that Messi seemed to have stopped growing. While other members of the Machine of '87 were getting bigger, Messi was not.

"SINCE I WAS LITTLE . . . I HAD THE DREAM OF ACHIEVING SUCCESS DOING WHAT I LIKED."

BEST LEFTIES

Although there is no distinct advantage—or disadvantage—to being left-footed in soccer, it's relatively rare for a left-footed player to be a star on the pitch. The website *Bleacher Report* ranked the best all-time lefties, and Messi ranked No. 1. His countryman Diego Maradona was No. 2, one of the major factors in the early comparisons of the two players.

One teammate remembered that when the boys would be handed their jerseys for the game, Messi was the only one who would turn away as he put it on. Messi was, he thought, embarrassed.

Messi had been born with a growth hormone deficiency, a condition that afflicts anywhere from one in 4,000 to one in 10,000 newborns. Left to its own biology, Messi's body would have grown to an adult height of a little less than five feet, but with treatment, he could be expected to reach somewhere in the range of a normal adult height. It was officials with Newell's Old Boys who first raised his case to the endocrinologist Dr. Diego Schwarzstein. By age 11, a growth treatment plan was in place.

The doctor remembered explaining the therapy to Messi and his family, detailing how grueling it could be for children. Self-administered injections would be a daily requirement for years on end. When Messi asked, "Will I grow?" Dr. Schwarzstein, aware of the boy's soccer ambitions—though not fully (yet) appreciative of his talent—recalled Maradona, who was just 5-foot-5 himself. "You will be taller than Maradona," he said. "I don't know if you will be better, but you will be taller."

Knowing his potential, the Messi family was determined not to let their son's growth issue hold him back. In the beginning, Jorge Messi (a steel factory manager) and Leo's mother, Celia, were able to lean on national insurance to cover the

STAT ⚡ When he was an undersized boy with a problematic endocrine gland, no one could see what was ahead for Lionel Messi. But if there is one number that sums up the greatness he has achieved, it is eight—that's Messi's total Ballon d'Or awards, the top award in international soccer given by the magazine _France Football_ to the world's best player each year. Only Portugal's Cristiano Ronaldo has come close to Messi's total: Ronaldo won five. Only 10 players in history (going back to 1956) have won the award more than once.

cost for hormone injections—1,800 pesos (over $1,000) a month at the time—but it was up to Messi to do the rest. As a child, he had to carry his syringes and medications around with him in a pencil box–like case:

"Every night I had to stick a needle into my legs, night after night after night, every day of the week, and this over a period of three years. I was so small that I was an 11-year-old with the measurements of a child of eight or nine or even less, and this was noticeable on the football pitch and in the street with my friends."

He was not yet a teenager, but the responsibility was on him. Messi saw only the payoff, and he was willing to do anything to overcome his physical limitations if it meant he could reach his goal. The injections were just another way to break down the barriers between him and his dream of soccer stardom. This would be one of the most trying phases of his fledgling career. He would later reflect on the stress of those early days, and the weight he carried as a young player:

"The last time I felt pressure was as a footballer with Newell's Old Boys, when I was eight years old. From then, I come on to enjoy myself."

"WITH HUMILITY
AND IN SILENCE,
I DID MY JOB."

£500,000

The napkin that Barcelona's Charly Rexach used to bind the club to a contract with Messi when he was 13 will be put up for auction and is expected to land as much as £500,000. The napkin, dated December 14, 2000, has the signatures of Messi, Rexach, agent Horacio Gaggioli, and talent scout Josep Maria Minguella.

MAKE THE LEAP

Beginning in 1998, when Messi was taking his growth treatments and starring for Newell's Old Boys, the Argentine economy began to falter. That faltering turned into a full-fledged collapse, with the nation defaulting on its debts, families struggling to access their bank accounts, and riots spilling into the streets.

The Messi family, like many, faced new hardships during this time. As the economy spiraled, insurance would no longer cover Leo Messi's growth hormone treatment. For a short time, Newell's covered a portion of the cost for their young star, and Jorge Messi covered the rest, but given the deepening poverty of the nation and Jorge's modest salary, that

was unsustainable. Newell's often tried to escape payment altogether, leaving Jorge frustrated and looking for new options for his son.

Messi needed a bigger, better team. He had to leave Rosario. He had a tryout with River Plate in Buenos Aires, a launching pad for many of Argentina's best players, but for all his brilliance with the ball, the team was put off by his youth and size. It didn't help that River Plate was in an even tougher financial spot than Newell's, and was not in a position to cover Messi's treatments.

It was lucky for him that while practicing with River Plate, he impressed some intermediaries for the agent, coach, and jack-of-all-trades Josep Maria Minguella, who had deep ties to the Barcelona

"I DIDN'T REALLY UNDERSTAND WHAT IT MEANT TO LEAVE MY COUNTRY, MY PEOPLE, MY FRIENDS."

Football Club in Spain, a longtime European powerhouse team. The moment when Jorge was given Minguella's business card was a pivotal one. It launched the young player into a new arena where he could get a little more attention and edge closer to his dream.

In the fall of 2000, when Messi was just 13, he was invited to his first tryout for Barcelona's world-renowned youth academy. His home country was falling apart, but here was a sliver of hope—a chance that he could continue with the medical treatment that would help support his career. Messi went to the tryouts and flew back to Rosario. For three tense months, his family waited on

Barcelona's answer. But Barcelona was a bureaucracy, too, and there was uncertainty within the organization about taking on an undersized Argentine who needed additional medical care. It was, finally, at the insistence of the team's technical director, long-retired Barça great Charly Rexach, that Barcelona agreed to bring Messi to Spain. Messi's dad famously signed the agreement with Minguella on a paper napkin over a few pints of beer.

Messi was thrilled to have made the team, but a little too young to be left alone in a new country. His whole family decided to make the move to Barcelona and stick together. They had always known that one day

Messi would have to leave his home country behind to continue on his ambitious path to the top, but that didn't make it any less emotional:

"Even now I can remember when we left our neighborhood and everyone came out to say goodbye. My mother and father and two brothers and sister were all getting ready to go in a taxi to the airport, and every single one of us was crying our eyes out."

Barcelona was a proving ground for soccer greatness. Messi's mission as a player was to show the depth of his skill to as many people as possible. On a personal level, though, he was a shy, introverted new kid, a foreigner without any friends. He was so lonely that he would sometimes cry himself to sleep after practice, covering his head with his pillow so his father would not hear. He knew he had to make it work and stay focused no matter how difficult and isolating it might be.

LIFE LESSONS FROM A LEGEND

- ⚽ STAY FOCUSED, NO MATTER WHAT IS THROWN AT YOU.
- ⚽ GIVE THANKS TO THOSE WHO BELIEVE IN YOU.
- ⚽ BE PREPARED TO MAKE SACRIFICES.
- ⚽ KEEP WORKING, ESPECIALLY THROUGH THE HARD PARTS.

GET IN
THE GAME

The leap from Rosario to Barcelona in 2001 was not initially a smooth one. Promises had been made to the family in advance of their arrival: The club was required to give Jorge Messi a job to satisfy Fédération Internationale de Football Association (FIFA) rules on international transfers, so Jorge had been told he'd work at the security firm owned by the team. Then there was the cost of the family's housing and the growth hormone treatments that Barça had agreed to cover. But deep into February, months after Charly Rexach famously signed the napkin contract, Jorge Messi had not been given a job and had not been paid. Team bureaucrats were dragging their feet on paying for Leo's hormone treatments, too, and the Messi family could not afford to cover the cost. It was only due to the kindness of one of Messi's supporters within the club, director general Joan Lacueva, that Messi was getting his medication. Lacueva was paying for the shots out of his own pocket until he could be reimbursed.

The truth was that within the Barcelona bureaucracy, there were more immediate priorities than Lionel Messi. Barcelona was in a lull, going from winning La Liga in 1998-99, to second place in 1999-2000, to fourth the following year. The more Jorge expressed his frustration about the situation, the more internal questions he raised about who was in charge, because, normally, few exceptions and indulgences would be granted to a diminutive Argentine who was years away from being a productive first-team player. The Messis had put their faith in Barcelona by moving there, but they quickly doubted whether Barcelona had put their faith in Messi.

In the summer of 2001, the family reached a breaking point. Messi's mother, who was deeply homesick, returned to Rosario with Messi's older brothers and younger sister. Jorge was tempted to do the same, concerned that the move might have been a mistake. He asked Leo if he wanted to go back to Rosario with him. They could search for another place to play—maybe again with

"THERE WERE MOMENTS WHEN I WAS REALLY SAD AND HOMESICK, BUT I NEVER THOUGHT OF LEAVING."

"I THINK THE MOST IMPORTANT THING IS TO TAKE ADVANTAGE OF EVERYTHING AND . . . BE AS PROFESSIONAL AS POSSIBLE."

River Plate in Buenos Aires, or with Real Madrid, Barça's Spanish rival, or elsewhere in Europe, perhaps Italy. But Messi was determined to weather the storm and stay in Barcelona.

Later on, he would reflect on how remarkable it was that his parents had left the choice to him, despite his age. He knew that their bold trust in him gave him the confidence to trust himself:

"It was me who asked to come, and I'm not so sure I'd have the guts to allow my own son to do the same thing. It was tremendously difficult for them, and I'm so grateful for all the encouragement my parents, brothers, and other relations gave me. Without them, I wouldn't be [in Barcelona]. It's as simple as that."

BUILD CONNECTIONS

The way the youth development program is structured at Barcelona, young players of all levels spend the week going to school at the academy known as La Masia. They practice after school and participate in games on the weekends. In his early years with the team, Messi struggled

"THERE ARE MANY TALENTED PEOPLE BUT MANY OF THEM DON'T MAKE IT BECAUSE, APART FROM TALENT, YOU NEED WORK, EFFORT, SACRIFICE, RESPECT, LUCK."

in school and, due to his shyness, struggled socially, too. He was brilliant on the field during games, impressing his new teammates with his skill and aggressiveness, but during the week, his teammates sometimes called him *El Mudo*: the Mute.

Messi lived in his apartment with his father, not in a dormitory like most of the other boys, which kept him separate from the team, but he joined his teammates in having meals and playing video games. "We couldn't believe how good he was," his teammate and friend Víctor Vázquez said. But it didn't match up with the insecurity Vázquez saw off the field: "In the dressing room, for a start, he was so shy. He would sit alone in a corner of the locker room before training, and then after the session he'd shower quickly and leave for home. It was normal, of course, after such a big change of life."

Thankfully, Messi's teammates at the time were willing to reach out and incorporate him into the group. "He was like the little brother of the team during the week; everyone wanted to look after him," Alex Garcia, the team's coach, said. The more outgoing boys on the team knew they needed to nurture him. "The whole dressing room agreed we had to do everything we could to help Leo adapt to living in Barcelona," Vázquez said.

"I'M A VERY, VERY SHY PERSON. I FIND IT HARD TO JOIN IN."

Thanks in part to their efforts, he began to feel more secure in his bonds with his teammates and even began enjoying himself. Now he looks back fondly on the rare connections he formed during that trying time:

"It helped me a lot because I came [from Argentina] alone, and I was with all the guys in the Masia, I was one of them. We were all from someplace else, and we helped each other. The truth is that there were a lot of happy moments because we were there together for a lot of time, and the relationships between all of us got stronger and stronger."

Years later, when Messi was the older player, the veteran star, he never forgot how he was treated in his early years. He made sure he reached out to the younger players who needed to feel encouraged and included:

"Off the pitch, I do the same things as ever with my teammates. As a person, I am the same with them. I am always

available to help anyone who needs help, though. I remember senior players being great with me when I was young."

PATIENCE PAYS OFF

As Messi and his father settled in and time passed, they gained a greater comfort level with the team, and the layers of red tape began to peel away. Jorge got his job and the paycheck that came with it. Messi's treatments were covered, which allowed him to focus on soccer and strengthen relationships with his teammates.

He was free to show those who doubted him why Barça was right in signing him. When he took the field in 2001 at Barcelona's Cadete A level, he dominated. It was so easy for him to slice through a wall of opponents with his footwork that the bulk of his goal finishes came on short kicks with no one to beat but a hapless goaltender. His teammates knew when to give him the ball and get out of his way. Messi scored 38 goals in 31 games that year. Eventually, his name and reputation began to grow within the club, and he rose up the ranks.

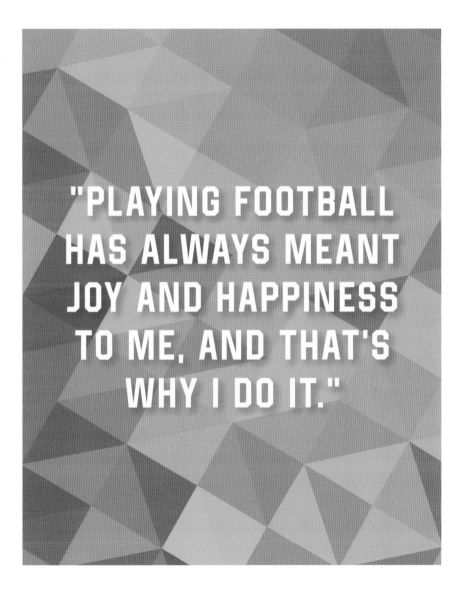

"PLAYING FOOTBALL
HAS ALWAYS MEANT
JOY AND HAPPINESS
TO ME, AND THAT'S
WHY I DO IT."

THE FACE MASK GAME

One game that has come to symbolize Messi's rise to greatness as a young player at Barcelona has become known as *partido de la máscara,* or the face mask game. During a match against Espanyol while he was 16 years old and playing for Barcelona's Cadete A team, Messi collided with another player and broke his cheekbone, suffering a concussion. Eight days later, Messi was allowed to appear in the championship game only if he wore a protective mask. He started the game with the mask, but it bothered him and he finally took it off and threw it to the bench, as his coach—who did not want to risk his young star's health—protested. Messi, knowing he was going to be pulled from the game, scored two mask-less goals in 10 minutes before agreeing to come off.

Even better, Messi's growth hormone treatments had started to work. At age 15, he was 5-foot-4. But one of the stipulations of hormone therapy was that he could not work out for extended periods. The lack of conditioning set him up for injury after injury.

By age 16, two years removed from the hormone treatments, he'd had time to take advantage of Barça's extensive training program. Conditioning and muscle-building were incorporated back into his training. Messi's body, at last, was catching up to his natural genius for the game. His youth career at Barcelona took off. He was moved up to the under-18 group. He played only three games there before he was moved to the under-19s. That's when he made his unofficial Barcelona debut.

GIVE IT ALL YOU'VE GOT

It was November 16, 2003, when Portugal's best team, Porto, the defending league champs, opened their impressive new 50,000-plus-seat stadium. They invited Barcelona to Estádio do Dragão for a packed-house match to inaugurate it. It was just an exhibition, really, so Barça left its best players back home, and manager Frank Rijkaard used the game to work in some younger players.

One of those players was Messi, known internally as the quiet 16-year-old Argentinian who had been dominating at the lower levels of Barcelona's development system. He was so excited just to be with the first team, and so were his parents. Both of them had come to Porto, and were seated in the crowd. With time melting away in the second half and Barcelona trailing 2-0, Rijkaard called on Messi to replace defender Fernando Navarro. He warmed up and entered the game.

Out stepped Messi, No. 14, the attacking midfielder who had starred for Barça's juniors, gifted with about 15 precious minutes of playing time. Shortly after taking the field, Messi had a golden scoring opportunity: a steal from the goalie Nuno, after which he got himself in front of a near-open net. He had more room than he thought, though, and rather than taking a shot at the net, he sent an errant pass to a teammate and lost possession. Not long after that, he was applying more pressure on Porto, slicing through defenders, taking a pass, and putting a shot on the net that Nuno stopped. It was enough to leave an impression.

Messi's parents teared up when their son took the field that day, thinking of how far he had already come and how much their boy had sacrificed for this opportunity. It had only

LA PULGA

The origins of Leo Messi's nickname, "La Pulga," go back to when he was an undersized youth, but whether it was given to him by his brothers or by a youth coach is uncertain. Either way, it caught on in 2005 when Spanish journalists began referring to 18-year-old Messi as "La Pulga" or "La Pulga Atómico." No matter how it originated, it suits the small-and-pesky Messi: "La Pulga" means "the Flea."

"YOU TAKE ADVANTAGE OF EVERY SITUATION, EVERY MINUTE THAT YOU HAVE."

been about two years since he'd moved 6,500 miles from his home to northern Spain, and, despite the loneliness and despair, the struggle had started to pay off.

After the game, Rijkaard decided Messi would be moved up from practicing with the juniors. "A player who comes on and in 16 minutes creates one chance, nearly scores, and is the man of the match, this boy has got to be with us," Rijkaard told an assistant shortly after the game ended. He would graduate to the Barcelona B and Barcelona C teams.

"I was very nervous," Messi admitted later that day, but he'd kept his cool enough to capture the crowd's attention. While most at Dragão that night were there to

STAT ⚡ In the 2002-03 season, Messi moved up the charts at Barcelona so quickly that he became the only player in club history to appear at five different levels in one season. He scored a goal at four of those stops, and recorded 35 official goals altogether that season.

STAT ⚡ **In October 2004, when Messi was just a little more than 17 years old, he entered as a sub for Barcelona, playing seven minutes in a game against Espanyol, a rival in La Liga. This would go down as his official Barcelona debut. At the time, he was the youngest debut player in the club's history.**

celebrate the stadium's debut, they would one day be excited to know that they'd witnessed Leo Messi's first appearance with FC Barcelona. It was a moment that would go on to become legendary, just like the player himself.

LOOK FOR MENTORS

In the early part of the 2004-05 season, when Lionel Messi was brought up to the Barcelona senior team, the biggest star on the team was the effervescent Brazilian midfielder Ronaldinho, who was at the height of his powers. Ronaldinho would go on to win the Ballon d'Or, recognizing the best player in the world, at the end of that season. Ronaldinho was aware of Messi's star power early on, and it didn't intimidate him. In fact, Barcelona players later recalled that after Messi's first training session with the senior team, Ronaldinho told them Messi would be better than him. He also recognized the budding young star's melancholy off the field, because he'd gone through it himself just a few years earlier. A 20-year-old Ronaldinho had moved to Paris to

"THE TIME I MADE MY DEBUT, THAT WAS MY DREAM COME TRUE."

RONALDINHO'S PREDICTION

According to Juanjo Castillo, a developmental coach for Barcelona at the time, Ronaldinho would sometimes comb Messi's hair in the locker room. When the developmental coach asked jokingly why Ronaldinho never combed his hair for him, Ronaldinho responded with a smile: "Because you're not going to be famous; he is. You're not going to be the best player in the world. He will."

play for Paris Saint-Germain Football Club, so he understood the fear and intimidation that Messi was feeling. Ronaldinho did not want those feelings to hinder the new kid. Messi usually sat with the other young players on one side of the locker room, while the veterans and stars sat on the other. "When he arrived, he was very quiet," remembered Ronaldinho. "The locker room was full of banter and jibes." He waved Messi over to where the stars sat and made space for him. Ronaldinho

wanted Messi to learn one thing from him above all others. It was the rule he lived by: *Play with happiness. Play free. Just play with the ball.*

Slowly, after spending a lot of time under his wing, Messi began to emulate Ronaldinho. He never had his easy smile; he never turned into the relaxed extrovert that his mentor was, but Messi did start to bring his own brand of joy to practice, to the locker room, and to their travels. As he began to get

"WHEN THE DAY COMES THAT I'M NOT ENJOYING FOOTBALL, I WILL LEAVE IT."

"IT TOOK ME
17 YEARS
AND 114 DAYS
TO BECOME AN
OVERNIGHT
SUCCESS."

"I TRY TO COPY LITTLE THINGS RONALDINHO DOES. . . . LOOK AT THE WAY HE ALWAYS HAS A SMILE."

stronger physically and mentally, Messi's daring approach to the game and ability to see the field became a joy in itself. He had a razor-sharp scoring ability that few defenders could manage, and a willingness to set up teammates for their own opportunities. The more he worked his style of play into the game, the more happiness and success he brought to his team.

A DYNAMIC DUO

Evidence of the quick strength of the Messi-Ronaldinho bond came on May 1, 2005, in the 34th match of the season for Barcelona, against Albacete. Messi had played sparingly in his first season with the team, but Ronaldinho knew he had more in him. Before the Albacete game, he told the young player that he would score. Messi

STAT ⚡ In 17 seasons with Barcelona, Lionel Messi established a club record with 672 goals. To put that in perspective, he has scored nearly three times as many goals as No. 2 on Barça's list, César Rodríguez (234).

came on in the 87th minute, replacing star Samuel Eto'o with Barça nursing a 1-0 lead at Camp Nou, their home stadium. Just moments after Messi checked in, Ronaldinho flipped a high pass to his young teammate, and Messi had just enough time to collect the ball and loop it past the goaltender for a goal. But Messi was offside, and the goal was disallowed. No matter. Just minutes after that, Messi and Ronaldinho were again out front on an attack. Messi passed back to Ronaldinho and darted toward the net.

At that point, Ronaldinho could easily have made his own run at a goal. As Messi later said, "He had so many different options at that moment. And he was waiting for me, to give it to me." Ronaldinho again flipped a pass to Messi. And again, Messi looped it over the goaltender, and this time he was not offside. It was a legal goal. The first of his senior career. In the post-goal celebration, Messi hopped onto the star's back, an emblem of how his teammate helped him rise up. He knew how valuable Ronaldinho's support was, and he was going to make the most of it.

LIFE LESSONS FROM A LEGEND

- ⚽ SEIZE EVERY OPPORTUNITY.
- ⚽ PUT FAITH IN YOURSELF.
- ⚽ FIND JOY IN YOUR WORK, AND SHARE IT WITH OTHERS.
- ⚽ TRUST YOUR TEAMMATES AND MENTORS.

STAY TRUE TO YOUR ROOTS

It was always important to Messi to represent his home country of Argentina and to be known there. Unfortunately, one of the consequences of his move to Barcelona at such a young age was that back home in Argentina, no one knew who he was. He had taken the youth ranks of the Catalan club by storm, earned a senior team call-up, and was beginning to make headlines in the Barcelona newspapers. But the last match he played in Argentina had been for Newell's Old Boys in Rosario in 2000. In his home country, Messi was out of sight and out of mind.

In August 2003, a group of Argentine juniors traveled to Finland for the U-17 World Cup. Messi had hoped he would get a call to join the Argentine side in the tournament, but the team's managers had not even thought of inviting him. They were not even aware of him. It wasn't

"WE KEPT SENDING THEM VIDEOS AND ANYTHING OF MINE FOR THEM TO KNOW ME IN ARGENTINA."

until after they lost in the semifinals to Spain that a videotape of Messi began to circulate among officials at the Argentina Football Association, the governing body of the national team. The footage was at least a year old. In it, Messi was 15, but anyone with an inkling of soccer knowledge could recognize his greatness. The youth team knew that they needed some fresh talent. They needed this kid Messi, but they'd already wasted valuable time.

While Argentina had until that point ignored its talented, exiled son, Spain had nurtured him. The Spanish national team had already made several attempts to persuade Messi to play a match for them. When word of this got back to Argentina, there was panic. Under international rules,

once Messi played a game in the jersey of a national team, whether Argentina or Spain, he would be bound to that team for the rest of his international career. It was crucial for Argentina to act fast if they wanted Messi on their team.

ARGENTINA, MEET MESSI

Just after Messi's 17th birthday, he got the news he'd been waiting to hear for most of his life. The Argentine Football Association (AFA) sent a fax to Barcelona requesting that Lionel Messi—which they misspelled Leonel Mecci—be released to his home country for a short time to play with the national team. The association had hastily arranged a friendly match with Paraguay. Though it was just an exhibition game that didn't count in the standings, this was a dream come true for Messi, so of course he was thrilled when Barça released him:

> *"When I was a kid, I expected to get a call from the AFA. I was asked informally if I wanted to play for Spain, but I always said that I wanted to play for my national team because I love Argentina, and these are the only colors I want to wear. I was always an avid fan of the national team."*

Messi arrived back in Argentina, was given a shirt that he'd wear with pride, and on June 29, 2004, after just a few days of training, he made his home country debut with the U-20 Argentina national team at the Autocrédito Diego Armando Maradona Stadium in Buenos Aires against Paraguay. It mattered little what happened on the field that day. There were, after all, only 300 or so fans in the stands. What mattered was that after halftime and with Argentina ahead, 4-0, Messi entered the game wearing an Argentina jersey, No. 17. He only had to step on the pitch to make his allegiance to the Argentine national team official.

"This kid is going to play a few minutes," said the game's broadcaster, with little else to say about Messi. "He's a bit of a mystery. He's 17. He's from Rosario, but he went to Spain to play really young." Instead of playing just a few minutes, Messi showed Argentina who he was. Late in the game, when

"I WANT TO BE AS SUCCESSFUL FOR MY COUNTRY AS I AM FOR MY CLUB."

"IT MAKES ME
FEEL GOOD WHEN
THINGS GO AS I WANT,
AND THAT'S HOW I LIVE.
THAT'S WHY I DON'T
HAVE ANY FEAR.
I AM BEYOND ALL THAT,
FOR BETTER OR WORSE."

Argentina had a 7-0 lead, he took a pass around midfield, sliced through two defenders, and easily beat the goaltender to make it an 8-0 win. After the goal, Messi couldn't help but beam with pride.

When the game was over, Gerardo Salorio, one of the AFA coaches, approached Messi. "OK, amigo, what's it going to be? Do you like playing with us?" he asked. Messi was a little confused by the question. Of course he liked playing with them. He had been waiting for them to call him for years. He had been with them only four days, but his heart was already in it. "I love this team," was his honest reply.

STAY LOYAL

There have been harsh critics and fans over the years who suggest that going overseas made Messi less of an Argentine. The fact that he spent nearly a quarter of his life away from the streets of Rosario and the warmth of home might have caused Argentina to be less than loyal to Messi, but Messi never forgot that he was from Argentina. It was part of him.

"I feel very proud of being Argentine, even though I left there. I've been clear about this since I was very young, and I never wanted to change. Barcelona is my home because both the club and the people there have given me everything, but I won't stop being Argentine."

The culture Messi grew up with was something he nurtured as much as he could. In Barcelona, he and his father would find the best Argentine restaurants—the beloved steakhouse Las Cuartetas in the posh Sarrià-Sant Gervasi neighborhood was a favorite—where they could eat their best-loved comfort foods, like the breaded cutlet dish Milanesa Napolitana (he liked it best with chicken, because that was his mother's recipe).

When he and his young Barcelona teammates would ride the bus to matches, Messi would listen to funk-heavy Argentine *cumbia* and *cuarteto* music, and let them have a listen for themselves. He had followed the tremendous disappointment of the 2002 Argentine national team in the World Cup (they failed to get out of pool play) and the exploits of the U-17 World Cup team in 2003, the one that hadn't thought to invite him. Although he cared deeply about his home country, and they had finally begun to notice him, there were still lingering but unfounded doubts about his allegiance to Argentina over Spain.

Despite the refusal of some to embrace him as an Argentine, Messi's career with the AFA was off to a rousing start. After the friendly match against Paraguay in 2004, and another against Uruguay a few days later, Messi became part of the national team's plans. Still, manager Pancho Ferraro didn't know how much he could expect of a 17-year-old player when the Argentine U-20 team went up against Netherlands for the U-20 World Cup. At the tournament, Ferraro surprised the team by deciding against starting Messi, who was clearly one of its best players, in the opening game against the United States. Messi sat, sour-faced, throughout the first half as Argentina fell behind, 1-0. He was substituted in after halftime, but Argentina was unable to rally and ultimately lost. Ferraro learned

"I WASN'T AWARE OF JUST HOW BEAUTIFUL IT IS TO DO A LAP IN HONOR OF WEARING YOUR COUNTRY'S SHIRT."

his lesson and, from there, inserted Messi into the starting group and restructured the attack around him. With Messi in the starting lineup, Argentina won all its remaining games. Messi scored against Egypt, he scored against Colombia to open the knockout phase, then he scored and assisted in a big win over Spain (the team that had tried to recruit him away from Argentina).

Messi scored the first goal as Argentina upended the tournament favorite, Brazil, in the semifinals, then scored both goals to win the 2005 U-20 World Cup, 2-1, in the final over Nigeria. He won the tournament's Golden Ball and Golden Boot awards. Back home in Argentina, the exploits of the U-20 team were being tracked by the newspapers, and the teenager who was leading the way was finally becoming a bigger star in his own country than he was in his adopted one.

He returned to Rosario, exhausted but having experienced what he called "one of the most beautiful moments of my career." He was greeted by television cameras and confetti when he arrived. Messi had turned 18 in the midst of the tournament, and now he was suddenly a national soccer hero.

PUT FAMILY FIRST

When he'd taken the pitch for the U-20 World Cup, Messi was wearing a T-shirt underneath his uniform. On it was printed, in black block letters: *Para Mari-Bruno-Tomi-Angus*. When he was asked about the shirt later in his career, he said he could not remember how or why he had gotten it. But they were the names of his little sister, his cousin, and his nephews.

"IT WAS INCREDIBLE, THE RECEPTION WE GOT; I COULDN'T BELIEVE IT WAS HAPPENING."

"At the time, they were the youngest of the family," Messi said. When Argentina won, Messi had removed his jersey and showed off the T-shirt so that the image beamed back to his family on television and in the newspapers. No doubt his grandmother, who died when he was 11, would have been proud to see him use the biggest soccer stage he'd ever been on to honor the smallest members of his extended family. He might have been away for years, and he'd barely met some of those newest members of the family, but 7,000 miles away in Northern Europe, Messi managed to celebrate his family.

Messi's relationship with his mom, Celia, was also extremely important to him. The first thing he did after arriving back at the team hotel after winning the cup was to type out an email to his mother that read: "Mama. I can't believe what is happening to me. I have to pinch myself to make

---

STAT ⚡ Eventually, Lionel Messi was not only representing his country in international competitions, he was leading it. Messi served as Argentina's captain in 19 World Cup matches, the most of any player in history. Mexico's Rafael Márquez is second with 17, and Diego Maradona did it 16 times for Argentina.

"I HAVEN'T CHANGED MY VALUES, THE VALUES THAT I LEARNED FROM MY FAMILY. THEY'RE THE SAME ONES I BROUGHT TO BARÇA. . . . RESPECT, HUMILITY, COLLEGIALITY, RESPECT ONE ANOTHER NO MATTER WHO HE IS."

WHAT'S IN A NAME?

It's only partly true that Lionel Messi was named after the American pop singer Lionel Richie. Messi's mother, Celia, intended to give her son the more traditional Argentine variation, Leonel, but Messi's father, Jorge, assumed that he was meant to be named Lionel because both parents were fans of the former Commodores singer. Jorge filled in the hospital paperwork with the incorrect spelling, and Leonel became Lionel.

sure that I'm awake." Though the email was a close second to a warm embrace, sharing his win with his mom made the moment even more joyful. Later on in his career, when he scored during a match on her birthday, he lifted his jersey to reveal a T-shirt underneath that said, *Happy Birthday, Mom.*

After the U-20 World Cup win, Messi told a journalist just how much it mattered to him and his family:

> *"With my family we went through many bad times. But as they say, this has been like a dream for me. I still haven't come down to earth. It's something unique I will never forget. Winning the World Cup has been the happiest moment of my life."*

The win brought with it a satisfying feeling that he had made the right choice, that all the difficulty the family had endured was finally paying off. He was making progress in Barcelona, and his future was bright there. But winning the U-20 World Cup in the blue and white of Argentina had brought his family a level of pride in their home country that his achievements with Catalans in Spain could not match.

As Messi's fame grew, he found new ways to involve family in his work and triumphs, eventually making his father his agent and brother Rodrigo his manager. His other brother, Matias, would later run the Leo Messi Foundation. He did not, however, put his

> "IT WOULD BE IMPOSSIBLE TO GET TO WHERE I GOT WITHOUT SO MUCH ENCOURAGEMENT THAT I RECEIVED FROM ALL THE PEOPLE OF MY COUNTRY."

mom to work. Instead, he got a tattoo of her portrait on his left shoulder blade.

TALK IS CHEAP

One thing that's consistent about Lionel Messi from then to now is his aversion to public interviews and his avoidance of the spotlight in his personal life. Even as he became more and more famous, he maintained a quiet demeanor. Interviews were often uncomfortable for him. During one uncomfortable Q&A session early in his career, he told the Barcelona TV interviewer that he was out of his element in front of the cameras. His confidence would return when he walked onto the field: "When I get on the pitch I can forget everything, and that's where I do my talking."

He gained the respect of his teammates, but he didn't demand it. In 2005, Sergio Agüero was a year younger than Messi, and he'd just joined the U-20 team before the World Cup. Agüero knew that the roster would feature a rising star who had already been playing in Europe—he had seen highlights

"WITH MY FAMILY
AND FRIENDS,
I'M JUST LEO.
THAT'S THE WAY
TO KEEP YOUR FEET
ON THE GROUND."

HOLD ON TO HUMILITY

When he was 13 years old and still playing for Newell's Old Boys in Rosario, before he had gone on the Barcelona tryout, Messi was asked to fill out a questionnaire for the local newspaper, *La Capital*. The questions were simple. Favorite sport besides soccer: Handball. Favorite meal: Chicken with sauce. But one answer Messi gave was surprisingly mature. When asked to define humility for the journalist, Messi answered, "It's what a human being should never lose."

on television. But he didn't know which star or what he looked like. So when he sat for dinner with three of his new teammates, he asked them who they were. Agüero said to Messi, quietly, "What's your name again?"

"Leo, Leo."

"No, your name," Agüero responded.

"Lionel," Messi said with a laugh.

"And your surname?"

"Messi."

The others looked at Agüero and said, "You *don't know* who that is?"

Then, finally, it dawned on Agüero. He snapped his fingers and pointed at Messi. "You're that kid!" He knew then he was chatting with a star. Messi smiled. For Agüero and Messi, it was the start of a lifetime friendship. "That's where we first became friends," Agüero said. "A lot of people might have taken that the wrong way, but not him." Clearly the wavy-haired teenager did not look like a potential worldwide superstar soccer player, nor did he act like one.

"I AM MORE NERVOUS TALKING THAN ON THE PITCH."

"I JUST WANT TO BE A NORMAL GUY."

Years later, Messi was asked why he didn't engage in a lot of self-promotion like other top players. Messi explained that it just wasn't his way:

> "I'd rather people talk about me. I know what I am, what I did, and what I can give, but I keep it to myself. People can have their say. I don't like to talk about myself; I like to talk about the collective."

But there would be plenty said in the coming years about Messi. Collective and individual strengths were about to collide with a coaching change at Barcelona that would spur Messi to recognition as the greatest player in soccer and deliver for Barça the winningest run in the team's long history.

LIFE LESSONS FROM A LEGEND

- ⚽ HOLD TIGHT TO WHAT DEFINES YOU.
- ⚽ VALUE FAMILY, AND SHOW IT.
- ⚽ LET YOUR ACTIONS SPEAK FOR THEMSELVES.

UNLOCK YOUR POTENTIAL

For his whole career, he was always the skillful little forward with the ball attached to his left foot, the player who dodged his way through defenders and left them baffled in his wake. Now here he was in the 70th minute of what was arguably the biggest game in his Barcelona career to that point, the Champions League final against Manchester United in 2009, and he was about to show off a whole new skill. Messi finished a pinpoint crossing pass from Xavi Hernández on a header inside the box. Usually, headers are the domain of the 6-footers and the leapers. Messi is neither. But for this one, Messi outdid 6-foot-2 Manchester United defender Rio Ferdinand, knocking Hernández's pass across the box and into the net. He would later call it his favorite goal of his career. It was an almost supernaturally perfect play, from start to finish, which was fitting because this 2008-09 season—for Messi individually and for Barcelona as a whole—was magical.

"IT'S THE MENTALITY, THE FIGHT, THE EFFORT, THE SACRIFICE. THE ALWAYS WANTING MORE."

Fittingly enough, not long before this evening in May, Messi's coach, Pep Guardiola, had been asked about the lack of header goals Messi had recorded to that date—didn't he need to use his head more if he were to be truly considered among the world's best? Out of hundreds of goals Messi scored, only about 3 percent were from headers. "I recommend you don't test him," the coach said, "because one day he will score a header and shut you all up."

The Champions League final match put Barça ahead 2-0 over favored British powerhouse Manchester United. Up until now, he'd gone 0-for-10 against teams from the U.K.'s Premier League, having failed to score against a British team in Champions League competition over 10 matches.

The resulting win gave Barcelona its first treble, meaning they were winners of Spain's Copa del Rey, the Spanish La Liga championship, and the UEFA Champions League, the tournament that pits Europe's best clubs against each other. They'd never won all three in one season—only four teams in soccer history had done it, and none of them were Spanish teams. It was Messi driving the team forward in all three titles. He had scored nine goals in 12 Champions League games (he assisted on five others), and 23

"I THINK SINCE I WAS VERY YOUNG, I WAS VERY RESPONSIBLE AND VERY SURE IN WHAT I WANTED AND I ALWAYS GAVE THE MAXIMUM TO ACHIEVE IT."

"I START EARLY AND I STAY LATE, DAY AFTER DAY, YEAR AFTER YEAR."

with 13 assists in 31 La Liga matches. In eight Copa games, he had scored, improbably, six goals.

The Spanish newspaper *El País* spoke to Messi's dominance the next day: "At Olympic Stadium, 20,000 *cules* were heard chanting Messi's name, 'La Pulga' (the Flea). With [9] Champions League goals and every title in the bag, there can no longer be any doubt: Messi is the best." He was only 21 years old. But Lionel Messi was no longer a precocious rising star. He was a shining one.

EMBRACE CHANGE

After the 2007-08 season, when Barcelona slipped to third place, the club had decided it was time to move on, not only from Rijkaard, but also from Messi's mentor, Ronaldinho, and other top Barça

stars. Ronaldinho had lost focus, and wasn't taking his training seriously. Though he and Messi had become close, the upside of sending Ronaldinho off to A.C. Milan of the Italian league was that the team could finally be given over to Messi, who welcomed the challenge.

Pep Guardiola took the reins at Barcelona in the 2008-09 season at the age of 37 with limited experience—he had been the Barcelona B-team manager. Guardiola's task, as he saw it, was to unleash Messi. But the young coach first had to gain Messi's trust. There was some bitterness toward club management over Ronaldinho's departure, and for Messi, that bitterness only grew when Barcelona barred Messi from playing for Argentina's national team in the 2008 Beijing Olympics.

Guardiola made some moves to put himself in Messi's corner. First, he stepped in on Messi's behalf to insist that the club allow him to play for Argentina. Second, he used flattery.

There was no question that Messi had gotten better and better in his first four years with Barcelona, but from the very first press conference, Guardiola dubbed him the best player on the team (which was accepted truth) and referred to him as the best in the world (which was not yet true). If Messi heard him say that enough, Guardiola figured, he would make it his goal to play like it. "Messi is a player at another level," Guardiola said of the young star. "The difference is in his head, in his competitive soul. When he's happy, things go his way."

While those two approaches initially ingratiated Guardiola to Messi, what bonded the two was their attention to detail and their perfectionism. Guardiola was a meticulous watcher of film and kept detailed reports on opposing players and teams. He was open to employing the kind of cutting-edge advanced statistics that a stuffy century-old club mostly scorned.

Guardiola had a knack for finding small weaknesses in opponents and adapting different ways—sometimes minor, sometimes major—to exploit them. They would watch video together late into the night and make adjustments in order to create just a bit more space. Messi knew the value of even a few extra yards. As Messi started to see the benefit

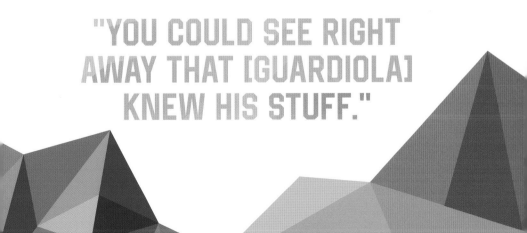

"YOU COULD SEE RIGHT AWAY THAT [GUARDIOLA] KNEW HIS STUFF."

of his coach's adjustments during matches, he began to fully trust the new coach:

> *"Everything he planned always ended up happening. He is special in the way he sees things, prepares for matches, and communicates."*

Guardiola leveraged that trust in order to implement additional changes in Messi's approach to the game. The first change was related to his health. Messi had suffered hamstring injuries and a foot fracture early in his career with the senior team, and they had held him back from reaching his full potential. Guardiola wanted Messi to be smarter about conditioning and more serious about his diet, which had remained unchanged since he arrived in Spain as a teenager. His top foods included pizza, Coke, Sprite, Milanese napolitana, hot dogs, and McDonald's. One of Guardiola's first symbolic acts as manager was to have the soda machine near the locker room removed.

Guardiola saw to it that Messi was assigned a nutritionist. Once a notoriously picky eater, Messi started to try new, healthier foods. For the first time in his life, he was eating fish. Guardiola brought the budding field of

"I LEARNED TO PLAY TACTICALLY, WHICH IS WHAT I MOST NEEDED, WHAT MY GAME NEEDED."

sports science to the team. He urged Messi to take naps, and he underscored the importance of rest. He taught Messi the benefits of holding back and conserving oneself throughout a match instead of going full speed all the time. He taught him how to maximize his muscle type. Messi was open to these insights and eager to see how they might improve his game:

"Guardiola has something special about him. . . . He makes you see things in a certain way, in terms of how he prepares for games, both defensively and going forward. He could tell you exactly how the match is going and how you have to attack to win."

With three championship trophies in one season—Guardiola's first as a coach and Messi's first as an undisputed leading man—this was clearly a winning combo with a common philosophy. There was always room for growth:

"The day you think there are no improvements to be made is a sad one for any player."

CONSIDER YOUR TEAM

Becoming a more tactical player was one of the first changes in Messi at age 21. From his days at Newell's Old Boys, Messi was always ready to take on all comers in 1-on-11 fashion, and he had so much pure talent, he could often win that way. For the first four years of his Barcelona career, Messi's job was mainly to score goals. But as brilliant as his left foot was, it was time to start using his right foot more. It was also time to take a broader approach:

"I THINK MY [SUCCESS COMES FROM MY] DESIRE TO ALWAYS GET BETTER, TO ALWAYS WANT MORE, TO ALWAYS BE MY TOP CRITIC, AND ACCEPTING THE GOOD AND THE BAD."

"EVERY YEAR I TRY TO GROW AS A PLAYER AND NOT GET STUCK IN A RUT."

"Before, I used to try to steal the ball and make something happen on my own—or at least try to do something on my own. Now, I try to make the team play more. I pass the ball more and I try not to be so selfish, if you will. I try to move the team from one position to another. I still run as much as ever, just in a different way."

This new phase of his evolution required him to see a match in the larger context, to think about the game beyond his own improvement and accomplishments. He had to build on his understanding of the other players on the team to make this work. That included knowing their skills, but also their emotions and mindsets. Guardiola challenged Messi to take responsibility for his own personal improvement, both as a player and as a leader.

KEEP YOUR EGO IN CHECK

After his remarkable production over the 2008-09 season, Messi was an easy pick for that season's Ballon d'Or award, which recognizes the best soccer player in the world. Though it was his first time earning the award, he received 473 points in the voting, 240 more than No. 2 on the list, Portugal's Cristiano Ronaldo. It was the widest margin of victory in Ballon d'Or history. Just to show what a remarkably high level the team was playing in that season, four of the top five finishers for the Ballon d'Or that year (everyone except for Ronaldo) were Barcelona players.

"PEP IS THE BEST COACH I'VE EVER HAD."

After winning the award, though, Messi chose to turn the spotlight back onto his teammates:

"To have the recognition of being the best player in the world is something special. It makes me happy and proud, but neither was I obsessed with the award. . . . It's well-deserved that there are so many players from Barça up there. The prize is for all the group, to the youth system of Barcelona because we have achieved everything with a lot of home-grown players. It's important for the club. I would've voted for any of my teammates."

Team trophies piled up for Barcelona in the years that Messi and Guardiola were together. The pairing lasted for four spectacular seasons, and in that time, they won the Spanish La Liga three times, the Champions League twice, the Copa del Rey twice, and the FIFA Club World Cup championships twice. In all, Barcelona won 14 trophies in that span, the most productive stretch in the history of the club.

KOBE AND MESSI

Ronaldinho introduced Messi to basketball star Kobe Bryant in the summer of 2006, describing Messi as "the guy who is going to be the greatest player of all time." When Bryant looked unconvinced, confident that Ronaldinho was the best, Ronaldinho disagreed: "No, no. This kid right here." Bryant and Messi later became friends, and they appeared together in a Turkish Airlines ad in 2012.

"I DON'T PLAY TO
BE THE BEST EVER
OR THE BEST
AT THE MOMENT.
I PLAY TO TRY [TO]
DO THINGS RIGHT.
FIRST OF ALL,
FOR THE TEAM.
THEN FOR THE PEOPLE,
AND THEN FOR ME."

Messi's own performance had also improved in his time with Guardiola. He scored 16 goals and gave out 16 assists in the season before Guardiola arrived, a fourth-place Barcelona finish. In their first season together, those numbers rose to 38 goals and 19 assists. He had taken his game, his team, and, ultimately, the sport in general, to a new level. Every year that Messi and Guardiola worked together, Messi's game improved. In 2009-10, he scored 47 goals and 12 assists. He scored 53 goals with 25 assists the year after that, and in Guardiola's final year (2011-12), Messi scored a whopping 73 goals and had 32 assists.

The changes that took place around Messi at Barcelona helped him sharpen his focus and made him

"THE MOST IMPORTANT THING IS THE COLLECTIVE TROPHY."

zero in more precisely on what mattered most to him, which was winning. There was some irony in the fact that he achieved the highest individual award for soccer greatness at the same time he had become more aware of the importance of the team. Or maybe it was not that ironic, because it was at this time that Messi grasped a full understanding that his individual success and the success of his team were interconnected.

LIFE LESSONS FROM A LEGEND

- BE OPEN TO NEW APPROACHES.
- DON'T GET TOO COMFORTABLE IN YOUR ABILITIES.
- WORK SMARTER AND HARDER.
- STAY LOYAL TO YOUR TEAM.

"I TRY TO IMPROVE
MY GAME IN EVERY
WAY POSSIBLE.
BUT THAT TRAIT
IS NOT SOMETHING
I'VE WORKED ON,
IT'S PART OF ME."

GROW FROM PAIN

CHAPTER 5

For much of the 2014 World Cup tournament, Lionel Messi did what was needed to push his team forward. He was the captain of the Argentine side, playing on the soil of his country's biggest rival, Brazil. His team was, perhaps, too dependent on him, lacking in the requisite overall talent to win a grueling tournament like the World Cup, but Messi had managed to steer them through the group stage. He'd scored a winner against Bosnia-Herzegovina, another winning goal against Iran, and two goals against Nigeria.

Messi set up the game-winning goal well into extra time against Switzerland to move Argentina to the quarterfinals, then somehow Argentina survived Belgium and the Netherlands, despite the team scoring only one goal in the two games. Now Messi, no doubt the best player on the European circuit, was on the biggest stage of his well-decorated career and was eager to bring a World Cup to his country, something that hadn't been accomplished since the spectacular exploits of Diego Maradona, who almost single-handedly won

Argentina the 1986 Cup. Messi was under pressure to repeat that crowning achievement.

In the final game against the Germans, with the world watching and three decades of pent-up frustration putting added pressure on Argentina, the intensity was undeniable. Argentina missed a scoring strike just minutes into the match and had another goal waved off on a pass from Messi because of an offside call. Early in the second half, with the game scoreless, Messi set up what appeared to be a classic run for him. He gathered the ball, leaving room in front on the left side, perfect for his magical left foot. These were the chances Messi typically knocked home with ease playing for Barça. But here, he stuttered a bit, sending a clean shot across the goalie box. The ball bounced harmlessly wide of the mark, though, a sterling chance squandered. He looked deflated. His entire team looked crestfallen.

It was not until well into extra time—the 112th minute—that Germany finally broke the tie and took a 1-0 lead. Minutes later, a desperation header by Messi went over the net and, about five minutes after that, he was fouled while making one final run toward the goal. He lined up a free kick, knowing well that this would be Argentina's last chance to equalize the match and still have a chance to win the Cup. Messi had invested all his focus and energy into winning this tournament. He was 27 and at the peak of his career, but there were

"I HAVE BEEN THROUGH MANY SAD DAYS WITH THIS TEAM. THIS WAS OUR CHANCE TO CHANGE ALL THAT."

reports that he was suffering from exhaustion, with his father telling the media that he was "heavy-legged." He had a long-standing issue with vomiting before and during matches, and this match was no exception. Physically, he had given his all for his country, and now he had one more chance to keep his home country alive.

Messi lined up the kick, hoping to put a shot on goal, desperate to tie the match. He took three steps forward, and he kicked the ball high into the night. It sailed about 15 feet over the net. It wasn't even close. The broadcaster's reaction summed it up: "No, no, no," he said. "No, no, no. It's gone away." Messi had accomplished so much for Barcelona. But here, playing for his national team with a chance to win the world's biggest tournament, he'd failed. To the media, he said:

> *"I'm very hurt at not being able to bring the Cup to Argentina. I am very angry at the way we lost, so close to the penalties, especially as we had the best chances. . . . I just wanted to lift the cup and bring it to Argentina. The pain is very great."*

For months after the loss to Germany, Messi could not sleep. He would stay awake, replaying the game, reliving his missed chances. In the years that followed, Messi could only rarely force himself to rewatch portions of that game. He didn't need to. The worst moment was burned in his mind:

> *"I am competitive and I feel bad when we lose. You can see it in me when we've lost. . . . I just retreat into myself and go over the game in my head: the things that went wrong, what I did wrong, why we didn't win."*

DON'T QUIT, NO MATTER HOW TEMPTING

For soccer players who reach the heights of global stardom, careers run on two separate tracks. There is the player's club career: their professional team, the one they come up with or to which they transfer over time. Then there is the player's international career, played in their nation's jersey. The pinnacle of international competitions, of course, is the World Cup, played once every four years among the best teams from across the globe. Generally, a player's club career and international career, though separate, run on parallel tracks.

Not for Lionel Messi. While his club career at Barcelona had been a superhighway from the get-go, his international career with Argentina was mostly a dead end. He was the youngest player in nearly a century to make his debut for the Argentine national team in the 2006 World Cup at age 18, but he was primarily used as a supersub off the bench in that tournament. He sat out the entire quarterfinal against Germany, a game the Argentines lost on penalty kicks. Worse, Messi was photographed sulking on the bench looking decidedly angry, his legs outstretched as if in protest. It was speculated that he was actually hoping for Argentina to lose. It was only later that Messi knew the impact that photo would have on his reputation:

"I don't remember the moment they took that picture, the one with the boots, because there were no substitutions left, they started saying that I didn't watch the match, that I didn't care, that I was elsewhere. That's where everything started. I did not think of it. It was idiotic. Yes, I was fuming because I wanted to come on, but I didn't want Argentina to lose because I didn't play."

In these moments, he felt completely misunderstood.

The rebukes of Messi only got more intense as the national team's failures mounted. There was the 2010 World Cup in South Africa, with Argentina coached by Maradona himself, a run that ended with an embarrassing 4-0 defeat to Germany in the quarters. The following year, in the Copa América tournament played in Argentina, the home crowd booed Messi and the national team. The 2014 heartbreak in Rio followed. Messi could take the fallout, but it became too much when his family was targeted. Looking back, he remembers wanting to spare them from the negativity and misconceptions:

"I AM DONE WITH THIS TEAM."

"I know that they suffered during the time when I was hated in the national team and they had to endure a lot of things, where day after day they turned on the TV and heard people criticizing me, or talking about things that weren't true."

In 2016, Messi was so fed up with the failures of the national team, the negativity toward him and his family, and his own inability to deliver international glory to Argentina that he announced, after a devastating loss to Chile, that he would quit playing for the national team altogether. A win just didn't seem possible anymore.

"Unfortunately, I searched for it, it was what I wanted most, but now it's over," he explained, relieving himself of what had become a burden.

But shortly after vowing to retire from the Argentine national team, Messi had a change of heart. It was not his style to give up, not his way. Few would have blamed him for walking away at that point, but he knew he would have to carry the disappointment of not winning for his country if he did that. The way to deal with criticism from fans of the national team was not to walk away. It was to win. That steady resolve was what defined Messi.

DON'T GO, LIO

When Messi publicly announced that he would no longer play for Argentina, he expected to get harsh criticism back home—he was used to that. But instead, Argentinians responded by pleading with him to stay. He was greeted at the airport with signs reading "No Te Vayas, Lio" ("Do Not Go, Lio"), a slogan that went viral on Twitter. Commentators apologized for their past criticism. Maradona urged him to come back, saying, "Messi must go on."

"SOMETHING DEEP IN MY CHARACTER ALLOWS ME TO TAKE THE HITS, AND GET ON WITH TRYING TO WIN."

THE SPIRIT OF MARADONA

Diego Maradona was just 60 years old when he died in November 2020. Messi, who had a complicated but loving relationship with his boyhood idol, lay awake one night shortly after learning of his death. Something, he later said, drew him to a closet where he kept some of his old memorabilia. When he went to it, to his surprise, the closet door was wide open, and an old No. 10 Newell's Old Boys jersey, the one that Maradona wore late in his career, lay across a chair. "That door is always closed, and I don't know what it was really doing there, I didn't even remember I had it," Messi said of the almost ghostly reminder of his childhood idol. He wore it under his Barcelona jersey in his next game, and when he scored, he lifted his jersey to show the Newell's shirt, his tribute to Maradona.

DEFINE YOURSELF

One of the problems that Messi had coming up as a player with the national team was the long shadow of Maradona. It is impossible to overstate the supernatural status Maradona achieved in the wake of his 1986 World Cup victory. Not only did he score two miraculous goals to defeat England, but the game came just four years after Argentina suffered a humbling and bloody loss in the Falklands War—Maradona brought his country the Cup, and he brought a wider restoration of honor.

No one could live up to the legend of Maradona, though every young player in Argentina wanted to. That included Messi, who wore Maradona's No. 10 whenever he could:

"For us in Argentina, the number 10 is a very special number because, you talk about number 10 and automatically Maradona comes to your mind, right? During our whole lives, those of us who grew up playing football wanted to be like him and though no one is able to be like him, that was our dream and desire, to try and copy what Maradona did."

Although Messi had taken a different path from Maradona, who came up through the Argentine soccer ranks before going abroad, Argentine fans endlessly compared the two and seemed determined to put Messi in a lower status. Messi left for Spain at such a young age that many of his countrymen accused him of being more Spanish than Argentine—this despite the fact that Messi chose to play for Argentina for less money and less fanfare. They wanted Messi to be the player who could carry his entire team on his back, who would run at 100 mph at all times, heroically doing whatever needed to be done—again, as Maradona would have done, but the game had transformed since Maradona was king. Defenses were more sophisticated, and the athletes were better than they were in 1986. Messi is known for taking the measure of a match in its early stages, sometimes not touching the ball at all for long stretches. Staying true to that style was working for Messi on the field, and he'd continue to do it, staying away from the action until the time came to make his presence felt:

"I have learned to adjust myself in a game and find that moment. There are times when I don't need to get involved, and then I wait for that moment when I think that is the right time to give that physical effort."

Not everyone liked that about his playing style. Some felt that Messi should be on the ball more, controlling the action. Even Diego Maradona took to criticizing Messi, occasionally in starkly personal tones. "Sometimes Messi plays for Messi," Maradona said. "It is Messi FC." He implied that Messi wasn't much of a leader. "There

"I'M NOT THE TYPICAL GOAL-SCORER."

"I PREFER TO COME FROM BEHIND, TO HAVE MORE CONTACT WITH THE BALL, CREATE."

is no point in trying to turn a man who has to go to the bathroom 20 times before a match into a boss," Maradona said after Argentina lost the World Cup to France in 2018 with Messi as their captain.

He was never going to be accepted by everyone. Maradona was loved for being loud, bombastic, and outspoken. Messi would always be quieter and more introverted. Late in 2018, after his World Cup criticism of Messi, Maradona called Messi to explain it away. But Messi learned to let go of the Maradona legend. He had seen Maradona up close, had dealt with him over the years as a coach and a critic, and had come to see his boyhood idol as a

STAT ⚡ One of the complaints that his countrymen frequently lodged against Messi was that he was not the same player for his national team that he was for his club teams abroad. There is some truth to that—Messi was not as prolific a goal-scorer for Argentina as he was for his clubs over his career. He scored 24 goals in 50 World Cup and Copa América matches for Argentina, a rate of 0.48 per game. Playing for his clubs, he scored 721 in 889 matches, a rate of 0.81.

great player, but a flawed man like anyone else. It freed him to realize that he could never live up to the Maradona mythology—no one could. Fans, media members, and players would always want to describe him in contrast to their hero, Maradona. Fair or unfair, he was wasting energy fighting the tide. He knew he had to define himself on his own terms rather than those set by others.

He hoped that one day fans would appreciate him for what he brought to the game as an individual, even if it wasn't always flashy:

"I've always tried to manage myself with humility and respect and the importance of wearing the shirt in this way. I want people to recognize that for me as well as the game that I've played on the pitch."

It was about showing good character and being the man he wanted to be; it was not about chasing another man's success.

LEARN FROM LOSSES

Even when he grew comfortable falling short of Maradona's epic legacy in other peoples' eyes and

"PEOPLE HAVE QUESTIONED MY ARGENTINE-NESS, ESPECIALLY WHEN THE NATIONAL TEAM HASN'T DONE WELL, BUT I LOVE MY COUNTRY DEEPLY."

"THEY'LL REMEMBER ME HOW THEY WANT AND THE WAY THAT THEY WANT."

defining himself on his own terms based on his unique skills, Messi still had to dig deeper and come to grips with the failures. Often, there is a tactical lesson to be learned from a loss, a matter of needing a better strategy. Other times, the lesson is more about just experiencing the pain of the loss, letting it drive you in training, and letting it give you a sharper edge in the next match. For Messi, he accepted losses in both of those contexts, and he tried, no matter the slings and arrows he was dodging from critics in Argentina, to lose with grace and dignity. But he also tried to improve his attitude and leadership abilities after each loss.

As Messi saw it, every game a competitor plays provides an opportunity for that competitor to get better. As he matured, he realized that there was often a thin margin between

a win and a loss, and if he dwelled too long, if he focused too much on the margin separating victory and defeat, he would miss the point—the opportunity to grow and improve.

"I fell a lot of times, but I always decided to get up and try again. It happened many times with Barcelona and more with Argentina. It was a message to my children and the young boys who follow me, who are fighting for their dreams."

The 2006 World Cup experience, after which he was criticized for his sulking and poor body language, showed him just how thoroughly he had to consider every aspect of leadership. The mere way a leader presents himself is enough to have an impact on how his teammates and the public at large view him.

"WHAT'S HAPPENED HAS HAPPENED, AND I'M ALWAYS LOOKING TOWARD WHAT'S AHEAD."

In 2010, with Maradona as the Argentina coach, Messi needed to learn patience—his personality did not mesh with that of Maradona, but he had to find ways to keep his team together despite the team manager's flightiness. That was a lot to take on at age 23. In the 2014 World Cup loss, Messi learned to shoulder the blame, since it was his missed attempt against Germany that sealed the Argentina loss in the tournament final. It became clear to him that a player and team can do everything right and still lose.

After all, Argentina had three quality scoring chances, but luck didn't go their way. One of his former coaches, Julián Camino, recalled how proud he was of the effort Messi and his team showed despite their loss: "He had shown that he could have won the World Cup. It was one of the best games that Argentina played." The win just wasn't in the cards.

After quitting the national team following the Copa del Rey loss to Chile in 2016, Messi learned to

A RUN LEFT UNDONE

In 2018, Messi vowed that if Argentina won the World Cup, he would run from his hometown in Rosario to the sanctuary of Our Lady of the Rosary of San Nicholás, one of the most important pilgrimage sites in the country. It's about a 40-mile run— no small feat—but Argentina's 2018 loss meant that Messi was spared the journey.

"YEAR AFTER YEAR
YOU CAN GROW
AS A PLAYER,
JUST AS IN LIFE.
YOU CAN ALWAYS LEARN
SOMETHING NEW.
AND SOMETIMES IN
THE MOMENT YOU CAN
REVEAL SOMETHING
IN YOURSELF."

"TITLES AND ALSO DEFEATS MADE US GROW. WE HAD MORE HAPPY MOMENTS THAN UNHAPPY."

control his impulses, to remember that he represented not just himself but his family, his hometown, and his country. Six years later, Messi was back. Argentina suffered four World Cup losses on his watch, so as a player and a leader, he needed to find a way to put the losses to some use. The painful sequence of defeats Messi experienced with a very disjointed series of national teams taught him that he needed to think beyond his performance to build a cohesive and connected group. He was the captain. He had to be true to that. It was not enough to be the best player and top scorer: He would have to strive to make every player feel integral and valued so they could create the kind of team chemistry that wins games.

LIFE LESSONS FROM A LEGEND

- ⚽ DON'T GIVE UP ON YOURSELF.
- ⚽ FIND A WINNING LESSON IN THE LOSSES.
- ⚽ DON'T TRY TO BE ANYONE ELSE.
- ⚽ MAP YOUR OWN JOURNEY.

ACCEPT WHAT YOU CAN'T CONTROL

On August 8, 2021, Lionel Messi walked out onto a sparsely adorned stage in the Camp Nou press room in Barcelona with a podium in front of him and the Barça logo behind him. He wore a dark blue suit and a blue face mask—it was the height of the COVID-19 pandemic, and Barcelona had not played in front of fans for nearly two years. But he was not here to play, which was what he did best. He was here to talk, publicly, about himself—one of his least favorite things to do.

Messi's wife, Antonela Roccuzzo, sat in the front row with their three sons. Dozens of journalists and members of the Barcelona bureaucracy sat around them, trying to honor social distancing rules, but packing in nonetheless.

Messi had vowed not to cry, not to get too emotional during what he knew would be a grinding and fraught session with the press. He was there to announce, officially, that after 21 years with Barcelona, he was leaving.

EXPECT THE UNEXPECTED

He didn't want to leave. But quirks in his contract and in the financial rules of La Liga made it impossible for him to stay with the only club he had known, the team that had nurtured him since he was 13. Any pretense of fighting back his tears was quickly lost. Before Messi could say anything, his eyes welled and he stepped toward Antonela, who was already prepared with a handful of tissues. Messi wiped his face, took the podium, and said, "Truth is, I don't know what to say here." He went on to try to explain what Barcelona meant to him:

"I gave everything for this club, for this shirt from the first day I arrived until the very last, and the truth is that I'm leaving. I'm so grateful for the care that people have shown me. I'd love to be able to go in a different way. I never imagined having to say goodbye because I'd never thought of it."

He did not talk about his many records, about the 672 goals he scored for the club, the most in team history and the most for any one club in the history of the sport. He did not talk about the four-goal games (he had seven such matches in his Barcelona career), nor about the hat tricks (36), nor the individual feats of greatness. He did not even talk about the 35 trophies he helped bring to Barcelona, which were all on display to one side of him. Messi talked instead about the relationships and the teammates, and the support of the fans and the staff at Barcelona. He talked about gratitude and humility:

"I DON'T WANT TO REGRET ANYTHING."

I'M JUST REALLY GRATEFUL FOR EVERYTHING, ALL MY TEAMMATES, ALL MY FORMER TEAMMATES . . . EVERYONE THAT'S BEEN BY MY SIDE."

"I will always be so humble and have so much respect. I want to say that to everyone at this house, for the luck that I've had to live so many experiences here at this club, so many beautiful things have happened, also some bad things, but all of this helped me to grow, helped me to improve, and make me the person that I am today."

He didn't dwell on the financial snafu on the part of the Barcelona FC that made it impossible for him to return (he'd offered to slash his contract, but to no avail). Instead, he talked about looking toward the future and living in the moment:

"Let's keep moving forward because this could all end at any minute. I've got a lot of players, teammates that say that can happen. And that can be very difficult because every day we've got the routine, we get up, we train, I play the matches. And not having that at Barça will be difficult. But [as long as] I can, I'm going to keep competing."

It seemed everything Messi did with Barcelona was memorable. He was honored six times as the world's best player and brought home four Champions League trophies. It gave him some comfort knowing

"ENJOY EVERY MOMENT, ESPECIALLY BECAUSE THIS IS NOT COMING BACK."

that those trophies would belong to Barcelona and its fans forever, even when he moved on.

EMBRACE CHANGE

After leaving Barcelona, Messi signed to play for Paris Saint-Germain, where he joined his former Barcelona teammate, Neymar, and helped the club to two French league titles. His numbers for PSG took a sharp decline, though, as he struggled to fit into the new system. In addition, he faced a knee injury followed by a bout of COVID. He scored six goals in his first year and 16 in his second. He was even booed at times—many times, actually—by the notoriously hard-to-please Paris fans.

He was less concerned about the PSG fans, though, and more worried about how his children would settle in. Thankfully, his kids eased into their new life:

"We were always afraid that the kids would have a bad time with the change. And it was the opposite. It was very easy; they adapted very quickly to school, to their friends, to everyday life. For Antonela and me, it was more difficult. I remember the first day we took them to school was terrible. We both left crying. Saying what are we doing here, what happened? We didn't understand anything."

RONALDO VS. MESSI

While most consider Messi the best all-around player of all time, he is not the top goal-scorer in history. That honor belongs to his great foil, Portuguese star Cristiano Ronaldo, who played for Manchester United in England before moving to Real Madrid—Barcelona's long-standing rival—at the height of Messi's rise to stardom. The pair were not exactly friendly rivals, but even though he is not the top scorer, Messi can say he ultimately got the better of Ronaldo because his teams went 16-11-9 in head-to-head matches.

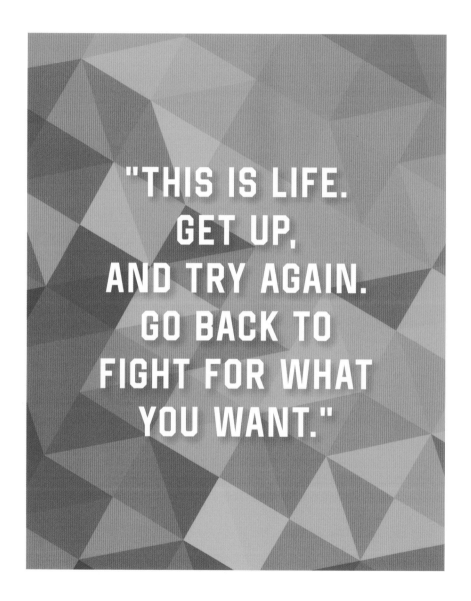

"THIS IS LIFE.
GET UP,
AND TRY AGAIN.
GO BACK TO
FIGHT FOR WHAT
YOU WANT."

SOCCER GOD

One of the nicknames Leo Messi has accumulated over the years is D10S, which is Spanish for "God," but with the "IO" replaced by Messi's No. 10. Pope Francis, a devoted soccer fan who was also born in Argentina, had some mixed feelings about the sacred nickname: "In theory, it is sacrilege . . . but I don't believe it. People can say he is God, just as they may say 'I adore you,' but only God can be worshipped. Of course, he is very good, but he isn't God."

The kids' flexible approach to change, he knew, was for the best. Leaving Barcelona was devastating for Messi. But his career thus far, the incredible highs and the disappointing lows, had taught him the value of stepping back and looking at the situation from a distance. A quiet thinker by nature, he tried to stay focused on the present instead of dwelling on future problems or concerns. After signing his two-and-a-half-year deal with Inter Miami, he tried to ward off questions about what would come next: "Today the most important thing is to enjoy what's left, whatever it is, it can be little or a lot."

In a discussion with French star Zinedine Zidane, one of his heroes when he was a young player, Messi gave one of the most complete distillations of his outlook on life, a thought-provoking response on his approach to being both a star player on one hand and a regular person on the other:

"When you have a goal, the only way is to go after that and fight for it, right? I believe that in the end, things happen and obviously, the journey is hard and you fall several times. But things happen for a reason, and in the end, whatever needs to happen will happen."

When you're chasing your dream, the effort you exert is more important than the result. Effort can be controlled. The outcome, as Messi puts it, "is secondary" if you're giving your all:

A WEDDING MINUS THE PRIEST

Messi wed his wife, Antonela Roccuzzo, in 2017 in front of 260 guests (plus a security team). Because no church in Rosario could fit that many people, the wedding was held in a casino. It was officiated by a justice of the peace since the Roman Catholic Church would not allow a priest to marry them in a casino.

"I believe you start to grow until you understand that it is a part of this, that it is a part of life, where you can't always win, where there are many difficult times. And people suffer this in their jobs, too, in their daily lives. . . . And things don't always happen as we want but always try your best to achieve your goal."

KEEP THE FAITH

Inherent in Messi's outlook on the acceptance of things as they are and the belief that events happen for a reason is his belief in God. He was raised Roman Catholic, like 92 percent of Argentines, and that upbringing plays into his personal and professional outlook. His faith can be traced back to his young days in Rosario, where, from the time he started showing promise in soccer, he perceived his powerful left foot as a gift. He does not chalk up that extra heaping of talent to hard work or practice—he was only four years old when it became obvious that he had a flair for soccer, after all. He believes it was something that was bestowed upon him, something divine. He had to work to hone it, no doubt, but the raw skill, in his mind, was a blessing that originated beyond himself:

"It was God who made me play like this. Obviously, God gave me that gift, I have no doubt about that. He chose me and obviously, I then did everything possible to try to improve myself and achieve success. But without His help, I would not have gotten anywhere."

"I NEVER THINK ABOUT THE PLAY OR VISUALIZE ANYTHING. I DO WHAT COMES TO ME AT THAT MOMENT. INSTINCT. IT HAS ALWAYS BEEN THAT WAY."

When he prepares for his biggest moments, Messi does not spend his time mapping out events, trying to predetermine how things will go. He accepts that he does not have the power to control events that way. Instead, he finds solitude in meditation and prayer, allowing himself to go silent so that he can talk to his God:

"I don't think I've done anything decisive to achieve success or win titles. It comes when God decides and chooses, there is no fixed time—it happens when it has to happen. I have always done [that] my entire life; I pray to God about everything."

In putting outcomes in God's hands, Messi gives up the illusion of total control, further sharpening his ability to react to whatever comes his way.

LIFE LESSONS FROM A LEGEND

- ⚽ BE READY FOR LIFE'S SURPRISES.
- ⚽ EFFORT IS YOURS TO CONTROL. OUTCOME IS NOT.
- ⚽ WE ALL HAVE GIFTS. TAKE ADVANTAGE OF YOURS.

"I DON'T KNOW
IF THERE ARE
ANY SECRETS.
I AM ALWAYS CALM
AND CONFIDENT
IN MYSELF, AND
MY TEAMMATES,
AND TRY TO STAY
IN THE MOMENT."

GO FOR GLORY

It was November 2022, and for the first time, the FIFA World Cup was being hosted in the Middle East. Even 8,600 miles from his home in Argentina, Messi was the main attraction. Droves of people came from all over to see the best player on Earth, now 35 years old, try to fill the one hole remaining in his résumé: a World Cup win for his home country. He had a head start, winning his first trophy for Argentina the previous year at the Copa América, where Argentina beat Brazil in the final in Rio on a goal by Ángel Di María. Messi scored four goals in that tournament, earning the Golden Boot award. It was a monumental achievement for Messi and the Argentina national team, his first breakthrough as the leader of the group. But that was the Copa, the championship of the Americas. This was the World Cup, with hundreds of millions of eyes watching them. Hundreds of millions of eyes watching Messi.

Argentina's 2022 World Cup squad was not the most talented of the four that Messi had captained, but it had the best chemistry by far, in part because Messi made sure as team captain that everyone felt involved and valued. It was a promising medley of skill sets and personalities, with a heavy dose of determination. Expectations were high. Yet, even with that momentum, Argentina started the series with an upset loss, falling to heavy underdogs Saudi Arabia by a 2-1 margin. At the time, Saudi Arabia was ranked 51st in the world, which made them the second-worst team in the tournament. Argentina, by comparison, was ranked No. 3. The early loss stunned the wider soccer world and set Argentina on a precarious journey to potential humiliation. If they didn't win every match for the remainder of the World Cup tournament, they'd be out. But Messi was prepared for this. He had endured enough losses on the big stage to keep his leadership position firm. He sent the group an email the next day to help them focus on what mattered so they could move on:

"We didn't have to throw it in each other's faces. [The defeat] was bad luck. It was about continuing to believe in what we'd been doing. We couldn't start to doubt. We didn't have to change anything. We just had to forget about what had happened and start from scratch."

In the same way that the Saudi loss tested Argentina's resolve, the two remaining group games amplified it. They shut out Mexico, 2-0, then did the same to Poland in their final group match. Messi was poised and calm throughout this stretch, even with his legacy on international soccer's biggest stage hanging in the balance. Messi betrayed no outsized sense of pressure and, as always, heaped praise on teammates. When the press asked how he was feeling, he answered, "I'm enjoying it a lot, and I'm happy that I'm able to help my squad make things happen."

"WE ARE GOING TO BE MORE UNITED THAN EVER."

"WE HAVE TO PREPARE FOR WHAT IS COMING, WE HAVE TO WIN, AND IT DEPENDS ON US. THERE ARE NO EXCUSES."

Now that they had made it out of group play, the Saudi Arabia loss was well behind them. Argentina moved to the knockout stage where the final 16 teams would face off in winner-take-all matches. Messi scored the first knockout-stage goal of his World Cup career in a thrilling win over Australia to move to the quarterfinals. There, Argentina survived a tense and especially physical match against the Netherlands, winning on penalty kicks. The semifinals were a bit easier, with Messi again opening the scoring with a goal of his own and helping to finish it off, too,

with a dazzling assist en route to a 3-0 breeze of a win over Croatia. That landed Messi and Argentina in a challenging but enviable spot: They would play in the final against defending-champion France.

As always, there was immense pressure on Messi. During his press conferences, he confirmed media speculation that this would be his final World Cup, meaning that if Argentina lost again, he'd never earn the most sought-after prize of his career. But if he was feeling the strain of his circumstances, he didn't show it:

"People have understood that this is something we have to enjoy. We did extraordinary things: the Copa América, the 36 games unbeaten, a World Cup final. Obviously, we all want to win it, but it's a football match and anything can happen. Hopefully, this will be different to Brazil [in 2014, the Germany loss]. I don't know if this is my best World Cup, but I've been enjoying it since we got here."

When the moment finally came, though, the rush of possibilities overcame Messi. As he took the pitch to face France in the final at Lusail Stadium, he broke custom. There, just a few yards away from him, was the Cup itself, dazzling gold under the lights of the arena. "They say you can't touch it or look at it or anything," said Messi. But he couldn't resist staring: "I saw it

there, gleaming. The trophy was calling out to me." He would spend the next 90-plus minutes trying to answer its call.

Yet again, Messi gave his team the early advantage. He knocked in the first goal of the final, putting the team up 1-0 with a penalty kick in the 23rd minute. Argentina scored again on a goal from Ángel Di María, putting France firmly on its heels. Argentina played with the same calm confidence that their captain displayed all through the days leading up to the game. Messi was at his best on that day, as he had been all tournament, playing for his country with more grit and toughness than he'd ever shown before.

But it wasn't over yet. With Argentina ahead 2-0, edging closer than ever to ending decades of futile

"IT TOOK SO LONG, BUT HERE IT IS."

World Cup attempts, French star Kylian Mbappé came alive with an incredible combination, scoring two goals within one minute to tie the match. Messi answered the challenge with his second goal of the game in extra time, putting his team up, 3-2. But with just a few minutes left to play, there was Mbappé again, ringing up a hat trick to tie the match, 3-3, just before time expired. That sent the game to a tense round of penalty kicks.

Two miracle diving saves on French attempts by goaltender Emiliano Martínez gave Argentina the advantage, capping France at just three possible scores. When Gonzalo Montiel knocked Argentina's fourth penalty kick into the lower left corner, the match was sealed. Argentina had won.

Messi raised his arms and, overcome with emotion, dropped to his knees. All the foibles and failures of past World Cups melted away and became mere background noise. Midfielder Leandro Paredes, who was just 11 when Messi made his World Cup debut, fell to his knees alongside him. Marcos Acuña, Enzo Fernández, and Nicolás Otamendi joined them. A small human pyramid of sheer joy piled onto the star player at midfield.

At last, Messi had won the World Cup. He'd done it for Argentina, for his team, for himself. It was hard for even him to believe:

> *"It's just crazy that it became a reality this way. I craved for this so much. I knew God would bring this gift to me. I had the feeling that this [World Cup] was the one. . . . We suffered a lot, but we managed to do it."*

From the relief he wore on his face and the sweeping emotion that overcame him, it was easy to see how much Messi had wanted it. Winning the World Cup for Argentina was the crowning achievement of his career.

SHARE YOUR TRIUMPHS

In the days following Argentina's epic win over France, Messi could finally truly celebrate. He was given

a hero's welcome that week when the team returned from Qatar. An estimated 5 million fans—one-ninth of Argentina's population—crowded along the team's victory parade route, filling the streets so densely that the open-top bus they were riding in could not move along the parade route. The massive turnout shut down the capital, and forced Messi and his teammates to abandon the bus and fly over the fans in Buenos Aires in a helicopter.

Despite the excitement and the media's need to get as many quotes from him as possible, Messi said very little in local interviews. On New Year's Day, two weeks after the final win over France, Messi posted a picture of him and his family, smiling, on social media with a message:

"A year ends that I will never be able to forget. The dream that I always pursued finally came true. But that wouldn't be worth anything either if it weren't for the fact that I get to share it with a wonderful family, the best one can have, and some friends who always support me and didn't let me stay on the floor every time I fell. I also want to keep a very special memory for all the people who follow me and support me. It is incredible to be able to share this path with all of you."

In typical Messi style, he shared credit and glory with those around him. He insists that he be treated like anyone else, reminds his fans that he has struggles like everyone else, and believes that because he

---

STAT ⚡ In December 2022, with Messi having helped secure the World Cup for Argentina, a trend started in Santa Fe, Messi's home province. That month, 49 babies were named Lionel or Lionela, a considerable spike from previous months, in which an average of about six babies were named Lionel or Lionela.

"YOU HAVE TO KEEP WORKING HARD AND PLAYING WELL BECAUSE PEOPLE WILL START TO FORGET WHAT YOU HAVE DONE BEFORE IF YOU DON'T."

has flaws, he's unqualified to dole out advice. Even after winning the World Cup, he stayed true to form. He knew that some might look to him as a hero or role model, but he didn't want it to go to his head: "I act like myself. I don't like to give advice or be an example," he said. "But if I have to, I am going to do it my way. I try to conduct myself the best way possible."

Messi isn't the guy who's ready with a rousing speech or who thrives on interviews. He's a man who is best sized up by his actions. During and after his chase to bring World Cup glory to his country, several unheralded stories cropped up that revealed one of the most important lessons Messi imparts: Be a good example to others, and abide by your own principles.

BE SOMEONE TO BELIEVE IN

Despite Messi's stiff interviews, members of the press warmed to him. An Argentine journalist named Rama Pantarotto once offered something personal to Messi during an interview. It was a red ribbon from his mother that he had been carrying around for good luck. He said, "My mum loves you more than she loves me; I carry her red ribbon for good luck. If you want it, I can give it to you." Messi smiled and accepted the gift.

Ten days later, facing Nigeria in a must-win game, Messi scored his first goal of the tournament to help Argentina win and advance. After the match, he saw Pantarotto. "I don't know if you remember," the journalist said, "but my mother gave you a ribbon." Messi smiled and said,

THE GOLDEN FOOT

In 2012, a Japanese jeweler took a cast of Messi's left foot, arguably the most talented foot in soccer history. The jeweler re-created the cast in gold, and the statue was then auctioned off in 2013, selling for $5 million. The money went to Messi's charity foundation, which then sent it to help victims of the 2011 Japanese tsunami.

"Look at this." He lifted his left foot, pulled open his sock, and revealed that he had worn Pantarotto's mother's ribbon for luck during the match.

The ribbon stayed with him as a lucky charm. Messi took it back to Barcelona with him after that World Cup. He presented it to teammates who were in need of a boost, including Brazil's Philippe Coutinho, who struggled in the early stages of his time with Barça. He passed it around to teammates with Argentina as well. Its final stop was the left wrist of Emiliano Martínez during the shootout phase of the match against France in the final of the 2022 World Cup, the one that secured the victory and the Cup.

Argentine journalist Sofía Martínez was also a Messi fan. She decided to break ranks during an interview session after Argentina defeated Croatia in the semifinals of the 2022 World Cup, setting up Messi's second trip to the final. As a reporter, she knew she was supposed to be a neutral observer, but as an Argentine, she had something personal to say to Messi: "I just want to tell you that no matter the results, there's something that no one can take from you and that is the fact you resonated with Argentines, every single one. Truly, you made your mark in everyone's life and that, to me, is beyond winning any World Cup." Her sentiments represented those of millions of Messi fans who were faithful through the highs and lows of his career.

"WITH ARGENTINA
I HAVE HAD
VERY BAD TIMES,
BUT I NEVER
GAVE UP
ON WINNING
THE COPA AMÉRICA
AND WORLD CUP."

Messi seemed to take her comment to heart. It was a reminder that the criticism he'd received up until then did not represent how all of Argentina felt about him. In a quiet but clearly emotional response, he nodded and thanked her. Martínez doubled down on her praise of Messi later, saying, "He is an example for all times in Argentina."

SHOW EMPATHY

In January 2023, Messi heard a story from radio host Andy Kusnetzoff about a young woman, Juliana Yantorno, in Argentina who had married her childhood sweetheart, Thomas. He was such a great fan of Argentina soccer, and Messi in particular, that he traveled to Russia for the 2018 World Cup to support the team. To show his devotion, he made up about 10,000 cards featuring a saintly image of Messi on the front and a Messi-fied version of the Lord's Prayer on the back. Thomas handed the cards out to every fan he bumped into.

Two years later, Thomas tragically died in a car accident. Heartbroken, Juliana had a hard time even watching the national team following his death. But before the 2022 World Cup, Juliana decided to honor her late husband by reviving his Messi cards, circulating them to as many people as she could during the 2022 World Cup. While the world watched Messi and Argentina realize their shared dream in Qatar, Juliana got thousands of versions of her husband's cards to fans everywhere.

"I AM A NORMAL GUY: I JUST PLAY FOOTBALL, THAT'S ALL."

A week after the World Cup victory, Messi heard about her ordeal and her tribute. Touched, he called her and they chatted over video. Messi held up one of the cards that Thomas had created and offered her words of comfort: "Here I have the little card, and well, I am sorry. But I am sure he is somewhere, and he saw me lift the World Cup."

The 2022 World Cup will forever be remembered as Messi's Cup. To everyone, that is, except Messi, who thinks of it as belonging to everyone who supported him or, as he put it, those who let him "share this path" with them.

BE FORGIVING

The World Cup victory left Messi with what he considered to be a complete résumé. He'd brought the same glory to the people of Argentina that he'd brought to himself and to Barcelona fans. It took longer than he would have liked, certainly, but he finally did it. Maybe because it took so long, maybe because he had suffered so much in international play before winning, the victory was that much sweeter:

"It is the thing everyone desires most. Everyone dreams big and the biggest is to be world champion with your national team. I was lucky to achieve everything at the club level with Barcelona and also at the individual level. This was the only thing that eluded me. There are very few players who can say that they have achieved everything and thanks to God I am one of them."

He acknowledged, too, that the rocky relationship with his home country could now be healed, since his critics had no ammunition left to use against him. Most of Argentina had already come to embrace Messi as a national hero by the time the 2022 World Cup began, but only after the win did he feel comfortable enough to declare it:

"I feel it is like a triumph for me to have changed that situation and won over all the people of Argentina. Today 95 or 100 percent of Argentines love me, and that's a beautiful feeling."

FORGIVE AND FORGET

In 2019, one of Messi's most despised defenders—Gary Medel of Chile, a player whose physical style earned him the nickname "Pitbull"—was at his peak. During the third-place playoff for the Copa América, Medel went after Messi during an out-of-bounds play, giving him a head-butt as Messi stood his ground. Medel was given a red card and expelled from the game, but Messi was shocked to also get a red card. Two years later, when Medel and Messi met again in a World Cup qualifying match, Medel approached Messi after the game to apologize for his past aggressions, and Messi buried the hatchet by giving him his game jersey. A photo of the two smiling together went viral.

No matter how critical and resistant the press had been, no matter how many insults his angry countrymen had slung his way, Messi couldn't help but fight for Argentina. And after he proved his love for his country with a historic win, he was also able to forgive and move on.

LIFE LESSONS FROM A LEGEND

⚽ STAY POISED, EVEN UNDER PRESSURE.

⚽ SHARE THE WINS.

⚽ FIND WAYS TO HONOR OTHERS.

⚽ DON'T BEAR ANY GRUDGES.

MAKE AN IMPACT

Messi didn't want to leave Barcelona in 2021— the move was necessary only because the club was in financial hardship and could not, under league rules, re-sign him. He had to scramble to find his next team and wound up in France, where he played two mostly unfulfilling seasons with Paris Saint-Germain. There was some success, as PSG finished first in Ligue 1 in both of Messi's seasons, but he dealt with hostile fans and a PSG management that did not treat him as a partner the way Barcelona had. When his contract was up, he wasn't interested in returning, and the team, which had suspended Messi for missing a trip, had already decided it would not renew his deal.

He was in talks with Barcelona, trying to find a way to return to the team he never wanted to leave in the first place. Those negotiations ultimately fell through. He had the opportunity to play in Saudi Arabia, where they were trying to build up their own league and were willing to give him hundreds of millions of dollars to lend his credibility and fame to the endeavor.

"EVERY TIME
I START A YEAR,
I START WITH THE
OBJECTIVE OF TRYING
TO ACHIEVE EVERYTHING,
WITHOUT COMPARING
IT TO ... WHAT I'VE
ACCOMPLISHED
BEFORE."

FOLLOW YOUR GUT

It would have been too easy for Messi to cash checks in a country where he would not be making a big difference: The Saudi league was insular, built only on the kingdom's massive wealth, and not on the passion of its fans. Going to Miami was different. Bringing his talent and his star power to a league that was still establishing its footing in the U.S. 30 years after its founding was something he could be proud to be part of. Leagues in Europe have long been better than MLS—which ranked 15th in 2023, even behind less-accomplished European leagues in Denmark and Switzerland—so it would take some real effort to build MLS's reputation. But it would be fun—something he didn't experience during his last few years in Europe. When he made the announcement, he did his best to explain his reasoning to the public and his fans:

"Soccer, you know, it became difficult. But I was always happy playing soccer and being able to have fun with what I liked when I was a kid. And today, I can keep doing it here, which was one of the reasons I made the decision to enjoy again what I had lost."

His critics scoffed. Some thought he was taking an easy path, choosing to play where the talent pool was weak and he could dominate. One headline accused Messi of turning MLS into "a league of old men." Another writer used a baseball analogy, saying, "Messi is basically getting batting-practice fastballs by playing against MLS defenses." Others said he was chasing fame,

"THE BEST DECISIONS AREN'T MADE WITH YOUR MIND, BUT WITH YOUR INSTINCT."

that he was following in the footsteps of previous stars who played in the U.S. in the twilight of their careers, all the while raising their celebrity profiles—players like England's David Beckham, who joined the L.A. Galaxy in 2007, and Brazilian star Pelé, who began playing with the New York Cosmos of the now-defunct North American Soccer League in 1975.

Messi shrugged off those assertions. He was not after ease or fame. He was after happiness:

"I made this decision based on a lot of reasons. . . . I came here to play, to continue enjoying football, which is what I've loved my entire life. I can tell you that I'm very happy with the decision we've made, not only for the sporting side of things but also for my family, for the day-to-day, how we've enjoyed the city, the new experience."

BE THERE IN JOY AND DEFEAT

Putting his career first helped Messi become the legend he is. But when he had children, career decisions became more complicated and demanded he weigh the benefits of family time and playing time. Just about every parent struggles, at some point, with establishing a good work-life balance that allows them to succeed in their employment and still spend the time they want with their children. It's an especially acute struggle, though, when you are

"I NEVER IMAGINED THAT SO FAR FROM SPAIN OR ARGENTINA, PEOPLE WOULD HAVE THIS AFFECTION FOR ME. IT MAKES ME VERY HAPPY."

a parent who happens to be a star athlete and global icon. From the birth of his first son, Thiago, in 2012, Messi vowed he would not let that happen to him.

Thiago's arrival changed his outlook, not just on his home life but on how he approached his work, too. The losses that used to crush him no longer mattered as much:

"The best [thing] I can do to forget everything is be with my children, wife, family. The rest is secondary. The arrival of my first son made me not just close myself off with football. I don't like to lose, to draw, but I take it differently. It's more than a result, sometimes you can't always win, there are surprises— you can't always win, and once it's over, there are other things."

His priorities had shifted, and the sport that had once meant everything to him no longer meant everything. Today, Messi and his wife, Antonela Roccuzzo, have three sons: Thiago, Mateo, and Ciro. All three are eager soccer players, but Messi is ambivalent about pushing them into his line of work:

"I would love for them to like soccer and continue. On the other hand, I know that it is a very difficult sport, that not everyone has the chance and the luck of going pro, that it depends on many things, and you have to sacrifice a lot. And that they also carry the burden of being 'the son of' and that, all the time, some people will be constantly comparing or looking for similarities to their dad. But in that sense, I think that since they were little, they've been prepared."

After arriving in Miami, Messi and his wife built their routines around their sons' schedules. Messi takes the kids to school every day that he can, attending their practices and games when he is able: "I try to be there in joy and defeat, and for them to be happy doing what they do, whether it's soccer or whatever they want."

"I THINK I AM A GOOD FATHER FIRST."

Messi still feels indebted to his own parents for the sacrifices they made for his career, how they fought to get him the growth hormone he needed and sent him to Barcelona so that he could have a chance at a career in the game he loved. He also knows that the most important lessons he learned from his parents were the daily ones, about the model they set for how to treat others and how to conduct yourself with respect. It matters more to him that he passes on those lessons to his children than his soccer skills: "I grew up with the values I was taught in my house. . . . And it's what I try to pass on to my children, and I try to instill and teach my children every day what they taught me."

BUILD A LEGACY OF HELPING OTHERS

When he was about 20 years old, Lionel Messi visited a Boston hospital as part of his American tour.

The hospital specialized in treating childhood cancer, and most of the patients in it were terminally ill. Messi happened upon an Argentine mother who told him that her daughter was a big fan. Messi met with the girl and was touched by her struggle. After leaving her room, Messi was told the girl's cancer was terminal. Journalist Cristina Cubero was there that day and remembers seeing Messi in tears as he left the girl's room. He hugged Cubero for support: "He clung onto me for four minutes, crying like a baby." It was a powerful moment for him.

Inspired to help kids like her, Messi established the Leo Messi Foundation in 2007 to help fight for and protect children around the globe. That hospital visit made childhood cancer his top priority. He was the spokesperson for a campaign to raise 30 million euros for establishing a childhood cancer

"OBVIOUSLY I LOVE FOOTBALL AND I LIVE FOR IT, BUT FAMILY IS ABOVE ALL."

"A CHILD'S SMILE IS WORTH MORE THAN ALL THE MONEY IN THE WORLD."

wing at Sant Joan de Déu Barcelona Hospital, which opened in 2022. When the funding was short by 3 million euros, Messi paid the balance himself.

Since then, Messi has found new ways to use his platform and money to help others. He was so moved by the devastation caused by the massive 2010 earthquake in Haiti that he decided he had to do something. He visited the country with UNICEF months later, and he became an ambassador for UNICEF. Messi met a group of kids who were trying to help rebuild their lives through sports, greeting each one with a hug and a kiss. "It surprised me," he said, "that people treat me in this manner and that I could get a smile out of people who have gone through such difficult times." Messi donated money

to provide pumps and nutritional supplements to help 2,000 children and their families in Kenya gain access to water and food. In a story that hit especially close to home for Messi, he learned of an aspiring soccer player in Morocco—12-year-old Waleed Kashash—who was struggling with the same growth hormone deficiency that he had as a kid. Kashash's family, just like his own, could not afford to pay for the hormone treatments, and his dreams of continuing to play were in danger of ending. But Messi stepped in and vowed to pay for the boy's treatments all the way until he turned 18.

Messi explained that, as he saw it, the level he reached in soccer came with a responsibility to help kids, just as he had needed help when he was young:

"IT IS IMPORTANT TO HELP THOSE WHO NEED IT MOST. I HAVE THE CHANCE TO DO IT, AND I'M HAPPY TO HELP AS MANY PEOPLE AS POSSIBLE."

"I reached my dream of becoming a footballer, and I want you to know that I fought a lot to get there and I have to fight even more to stay. I want to take advantage of that effort and that success to help the children who need it the most, because that is how I have chosen it, because I am moved every day that I get a child to smile, when they think there is hope, when I see that they feel happy. . . . That is why we decided to create the Leo Messi Foundation. And I will continue fighting to make children happy with the same strength and dedication that I need to continue being a footballer."

LEAD WITH HUMILITY

On July 21, 2023, in Fort Lauderdale, Florida, the atmosphere at DRV PNK Stadium was bustling. The home team, Inter Miami CF of Major League Soccer, had sold out the stadium for their game against Cruz Azul, despite not having won any of their last 11 games. They were in last place with just two wins and nine goals scored. But on this night,

basketball star LeBron James was in town for the game, as was tennis legend Serena Williams. TV star Kim Kardashian, too, was in the crowd. They came for the spectacle. Lionel Messi, the greatest and most decorated player in the history of the sport, hero of the Barça dynasty and the Argentine national team, was set to make his debut for Miami. He had signed a two-and-a-half-year contract a week earlier, and now he was set to be thrown into the fire with the worst team in the league. Things were about to change for Inter Miami, and for Major League Soccer in the United States.

Messi did not start the game. He spent the first half watching from the sideline as Miami took a 1-0 lead. He had practiced only three times with Inter Miami, so he was uncertain whether he should play at all. But his team needed him. This was a key game against the Mexican side, Cruz Azul, in the opening of the Leagues Cup, a separate tournament played between all teams in MLS and Mexico's Liga MX. All of Miami's losses at the start of the year were

"I PLAY ALL GAMES
THE SAME,
AS IF THEY WERE
ALL FINALS.
NOTHING CHANGES IN
MY PREPARATIONS."

wiped clean for this tournament. From here, Inter Miami would be Messi's club. At the beginning of the second half, Messi stood up and removed the red vest, signaling his entry into the game.

The fans roared their encouragement as Messi took the pitch. Miami captain DeAndre Yedlin approached him at midfield with the captain's black armband, a weighty symbol of leadership. Messi saw him coming and waved him off. He wanted to be treated like any other substitute. "I told him, he was the captain and I was OK with that," Messi explained. "He insisted, that, no, I was going to be the captain." Yedlin slipped the band around Messi's left arm. It was settled.

Not only did Messi lead Inter Miami CF to a win over Cruz Azul, but he helped the club to six consecutive victories and the Leagues Cup championship, an incredible feat for a team that had only weeks before been at the bottom of the MLS standings. When it was time for the captain to be awarded the Leagues

Cup trophy, Messi—stealthily—slipped the captain's armband back onto Yedlin, who protested. But now it was Messi's turn to insist. Yedlin relented, and accepted the cup. It was a moment of humanity where egos were put aside. Said Yedlin: "He could have come in and said, 'I'm doing stuff my way, and that's how it's going to be.' But he's come in and he's completely mixed in with the group: the old guys, the young guys, just like a regular player. . . . I have even more respect for him now. He's an unbelievable human being."

Messi is beloved because not only is he the greatest player ever to lace up his soccer cleats and play the world's most popular sport, but he's also an incredible human. Messi's accomplishments are many and wide-ranging: eight Ballon D'Ors, two World Cup Golden Balls, 44 team trophies and gold medals, *Time* magazine Athlete of the Year, and a Player of the Decade honor. From that talent, he has built up his own personal empire, with a net worth of more than $600 million and revenue-sharing stakes in such high-profile companies as Adidas and Apple, not to mention his expansive philanthropic endeavors. Messi is spending the latter part of his career working to cultivate a deeper love of soccer in the United States.

Lionel Messi has worked his way to becoming a global icon who does not just talk about his humble roots and difficult journey but uses that experience to connect with and inspire others. He took a passion for soccer and all the talent bestowed onto him for the sport and, through limitless physical and mental discipline, turned an ordinary life into an extraordinary legend. His devotion to his tight-knit family, the way he uplifts his teammates, the charity work he supports, and his lack of bravado—they all paint a picture of someone spectacular who deserves the accolades he's managed to achieve. For anyone looking to achieve a dream, rise above their circumstances, or live up to their potential, Lionel Messi's life is a lesson in boundless success.

LIFE LESSONS FROM A LEGEND

- ⚽ KNOW WHAT MATTERS MOST TO YOU.
- ⚽ FIND WAYS TO GIVE BACK.
- ⚽ BE THE BEST HUMAN YOU CAN BE.

"I WANT TO BE
REMEMBERED
FIRST OF ALL
AS AN ORDINARY,
REASONABLE PERSON,
AND NOT AS JUST
AN ATHLETE."

I HAVE BEEN VERY LUCKY

"**Thanks to everyone, especially my teammates.** Thank you to everyone who voted for me. This Ballon d'Or is a great gift for all of Argentina. I don't want to forget Haaland or Mbappé, who had a great year, spectacular, and in the coming years they will win this award. The level [of competition] never decreases; I have been lucky to be here for many years. I want to provide a special mention for all those people who were happy that Argentina became world champions. Thanks also to all my family, my wife, my children, for being there in the worst moments, and they have helped me fulfill my dreams in football. Without you it would not have been possible. I want to make one last mention of Maradona. Happy birthday: I think there is no better place than here to congratulate him, full of players and with a ball. This Ballon d'Or is also yours and that of all of Argentina. All the awards have been special, but I always emphasize the importance of the team. This is secondary. Look at City, they have been the best and achieved everything last season. I have been very lucky, I have played for the best team in the world, the best in history, I have been able to win many individual awards thanks to that. With Argentina I have had very bad times, but I never gave up on winning the Copa América and World Cup, and that's why I'm proud of not having given up."

—*LIONEL MESSI, Ballon d'Or acceptance speech, October 30, 2023*

MAKE THE RIGHT IMPRESSION

One measure of a person is the impact they make on others who know them best. Messi changed the game and people's lives forever, and it's clear in the way his coaches, teammates, sportscasters, and fellow legends talk about him.

Sports commentator Gary Neville: *"During his whole career, he's lit up every game he's played in. If you've watched Lionel Messi play live, you are truly blessed."*

NBA star Kobe Bryant: *"I wear the number 10 jersey for the US National Team in honor of the greatest athlete I have ever seen: Messi."*

Former player and commentator Ray Hudson: *"They tell me that all men are equal in God's eyes; this player makes you seriously think about those words."*

Former teammate Carles Puyol: *"He's well above anything else I've ever seen. He's an alien."*

Former Barcelona manager Pep Guardiola: *"Don't write about him, don't try to describe him. Just watch him."*

Former Argentina teammate Javier Mascherano: *"Although he may not be human, it's good that Messi still thinks he is."*

Former Argentina coach Carlos Bilardo: *"Messi defies the laws of anatomy. He must have an extra bone in his ankle."*

Spanish manager Miguel Ángel Lotina: *"Messi is Messi and others, footballers."*

RESOURCES

MAGAZINES/WEBSITES/ NEWSPAPERS

"80% of Messi's Growth Was Achieved Here, in Argentina," *Mundo Deportivo*, December 17, 2022

"Argentina Inspired by World Cup Anthem," *SkySports.com*, December 19, 2022

"Ballon d'Or 2023: Lionel Messi Wins Record-Extending Eighth Award," *SkySports.com*, October 31, 2023

"Barcelona Initially Unconvinced That Leo Messi Would Succeed as a Pro," *SI.com*, February 6, 2012

"'Bulls*** Referees', World Cup Heartbreak and Penalty Nightmares: How Lionel Messi Has Had to Endure Failure After Failure with Argentina," *Daily Mail*, July 3, 2019

"The Burden of Being Messi," *The New York Times*, June 5, 2014

"How Argentina Won the 2022 World Cup, in Their Own Words," *ESPN.com*, December 18, 2023

"How Ronaldinho Helped Shape Messi's Career," *FIFA.com*, December 19, 2022

"Interview: Lionel Messi on His Sport, Cristiano Ronaldo — and Argentina," *Time* magazine, January 26, 2012

"Interview with Lionel Messi at Age 13 Goes Viral: The Bible, 'Baby's Day Out,' Chicken with Sauce," *ESPN.com*, April 19, 2017

"'It Was God Who Made Me Play Like This'— the Christian Faith of Lionel Messi," *Premier Christianity Magazine*, December 20, 2022

"Lionel Messi at Barcelona: The Pain and Glory of a 20-Year Love Affair," *The Athletic*, July 18, 2023

"Lionel Messi: Boy Genius," *The New York Times*, May 21, 2011

"Lionel Messi: 'I Try Not to Be So Selfish' and More of a Team Player," *ESPN.com*, March 17, 2018

"Lionel Messi: The World at His Feet," *SI.com*, May 31, 2010

"Lionel Messi's Barcelona Debut: Oral History of Those Who Saw Him First, 15 Years Ago, vs. Espanyol," *ESPN.com*, October 16, 2019

"Lionel Messi's Rise to Greatness," *ESPN.com*, February 22, 2012

"The Love Story That Moved Lionel Messi: After Her Husband Died She Made Sure to Fulfill His Dream," *CNN.com*, December 28, 2023

"Messi: If I Don't Touch the Ball for Too Long I Can Leave a Game," *Marca.com*, October 27, 2019

"Messi: I Would Have Liked Maradona to Give Me the World Cup," *FIFA.com*, December 18, 2022

"Messi Reveals How He Solved Vomiting Problem with Barcelona & Argentina," *Sportingnews.com*, March 19, 2018

"Messi, Rosario and Newell's: The Love Between a Superstar, His Hometown and Boyhood Club," *The Athletic*, July 17, 2023

"On and Off the Pitch, Messi an Instant Hit in Miami," *AFP.com*, July 25, 2023

"Ronaldinho on Mentoring Lionel Messi at Barcelona: 'We Knew at 17 He'd Be the Best'," *The Athletic*, October 31, 2023

"SKY IS THE LIMIT: What Is the Meaning Behind Lionel Messi's Trademark 'Point to the Sky' Celebration?" *TalkSport.com*, December 18, 2022

"That Didn't Take Long! Lionel Messi Set to Be Named Inter Miami Captain After Just One Appearance for the MLS Club," *GOAL.com*, July 24, 2023

BOOKS

Angels with Dirty Faces, by Jonathan Wilson

The Barcelona Complex, by Simon Kuper

Messi: A Biography, by Leonardo Faccio

Messi: The Must-Read Biography of the World Cup Champion, by Guillem Balagué

PODCASTS/INTERVIEWS/ VIDEO CONTENT

"Captains of the World," *Netflix,* December 30, 2023

"The Happiest Man in the World," *FIFA,* December 2022

"Interview with Leo Messi in La Masia," *FC Barcelona,* February 1, 2016

"The Last Cup Podcast," *NPR,* November 2, 2022

"The Life of the 16-Year-Old Lionel Messi," *ESPN,* December 2003

Leo Messi interview, "Winning the cup was a turning point" *FC Barcelona,* May 22, 2021

"Lionel Messi Latest Full Interview" *Sone Que Volaba,* September 22, 2023

"Lionel Messi: The Greatest," *Entertain Me Productions,* March 3, 2020

"Messi Arrives in Barcelona," *Barcatvplus.com,* 2001

"Messi Meets America," *Apple TV+,* October 11, 2023

"Messi's Farewell Press Conference," *beIN Sports,* August 8, 2021

"Messi's World Cup: The Rise of a Legend," *Apple TV+,* February 21, 2024

"This Was an Unforgettable Day," *Unisport,* January 25, 2019

"When Zinedine Zidane Met Lionel Messi," *Adidas,* November 9, 2023

"'You Don't Know Who That Is?'— When Sergio Aguero First Met Lionel Messi," *Sky Sports Retro,* December 9, 2020

STATISTICAL WEBSITES

"Lionel Messi" *Fbref.com*

"Lionel Messi" *FCBarcelona.com*